INSIGHT *Pocket* GUIDES

ISTANBUL

101 Tourists & Visitors to

APA PUBLICATIONS

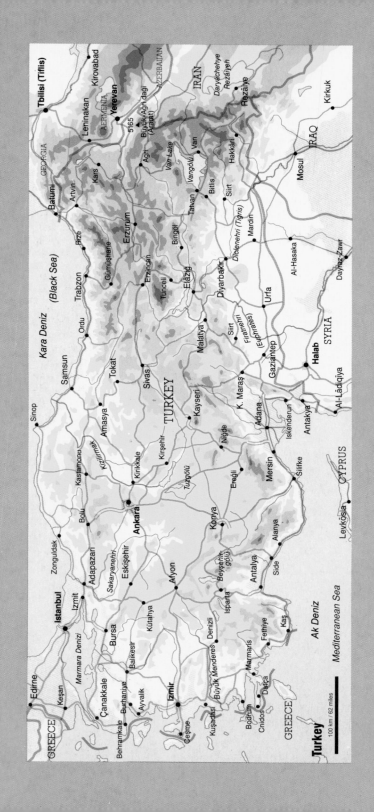

Dear Visitor!

Istanbul is one of the great cities of the world. Built on the banks of the Bosphorus, a strategic waterway linking the Sea of Marmara and the Black Sea, it has been the capital of three world empires – the Roman, Byzantine and Ottoman – and is filled with the riches of its past. But Istanbul is more than its Byzantine churches and Ottoman mosques and palaces; it is also a vibrant modern metropolis.

In these pages Insight Guides' correspondent in Istanbul, Metin Demirsar, brings you the best of the city in a series of carefully crafted itineraries. He begins with four full-day tours linking the must-see attractions, such as the Blue Mosque, Hagia Sophia, Topkapı Palace, and a boat ride along the Bosphorus. These are followed by five optional itineraries, designed to suit a range of tastes from haggling for bargains in the Covered Bazaar to touring the sacred district of Eyüp along the Golden Horn. All the itineraries include detailed directions on getting around and stops for rest and refreshment.

 Metin Demirsar has lived in Istanbul for over 20 years. He revels in the city's history and legends which nudge visitors and residents at every turn, pointing to the fact that in merely taking one of the noisy little ferry boats up the Bosphorus for a seafood supper along its shores you are travelling in the legendary footsteps of Jason and the Argonauts in search of the Golden Fleece. In *Insight Pocket Guide: Istanbul* he invites readers to experience Istanbul through the eyes of a native.

Hans Höfer
Publisher, Insight Guides

C O N T E N T S

Pages 2/3:
The Egyptian
Obelisk and
minarets

Pages 8/9
pillow merchant

Located on overland trade routes linking Europe and Asia, and on sea lanes connecting the Black Sea with the Mediterranean, Istanbul has been one of the world's most important commercial centres for some 2,700 years. It has had a rich and varied history, replete with myths, pageantry, military conquests, bloody political riots, bitter religious feuds, destructive fires, epidemics and earthquakes.

It has been known by various names. The Vikings, whose navies once besieged the city but failed to breach its walls, described it as Mickligarth, 'the Great Enclosure'. To the Slavs of central Europe it was known as Tsargrad, 'Caesar's City'. The Romans called it 'New Rome' because it was modelled after their capital.

City of the Blind

The earliest written records of Istanbul say it was founded by Megarian King Byzas in 666 BC, although archaeologists suggest

The Old City

the shores of the Bosphorus may have been settled as early as 3000 BC. Byzas, according to legends, consulted an oracle to help him locate the site for his new settlement. In a cryptic pronouncement, the oracle told him to construct his new town 'across from the city of the blind' When Byzas reached the Bosphorus during his journeys, he discovered a small Megarian settlement standing on its Asian shores, at what is present-day Kadıköy. These early settlers, Byzas argued, had been so blind they had overlooked the most obvious setting and strategic site in the area for colonisation – the hill on the European shore where the present Topkapı Palace stands, which has a stunning view of the Bosphorus, the Golden Horn and the Sea of Marmara. Byzas built his town on this hill and named it Byzantium.

Persian Domination

In 512 BC, the Persians, under Darius, occupied the town. Darius built a bridge of boats at the narrowest point of the Bosphorus to transport his army of 700,000 men in his unsuccessful bid to conquer eastern Europe. Persian domination ended in 479 BC when the city reverted to Greek rule under Pausanias of Sparta.

Byzantium repulsed an invasion of Celtic tribes, known as the Galatians or Gauls, in 279 BC, but agreed to pay a tribute to them nevertheless. Some of these blond, blue-eyed Celts settled in Byzantium. The harbour district which lies directly across the old city on the Golden Horn has been known ever since as Galata after these Celtic warriors.

In 179 BC, Rhodes, Pergamum and Bithynia joined forces to capture the city. Byzantium eventually became part of the Roman Empire after the Roman legions defeated renegade Mithridates, king of the Pontus.

After Byzantium sided with rebels in a Roman civil war, Emperor Septimius Severus sacked the city in AD 193 to punish the insurgents, slaughtering most of its inhabitants or sending them off to enforced slavery. He rebuilt and repopulated the city, naming it Augusta Antonina in honour of his son Antonius Bassianus, better known as Caracalla.

Constantine the Great

During another power struggle, the city capitulated to the Roman Emperor Constantine the Great in 324, beginning the Byzantine period which was to last more than 11 centuries. In two of the most important developments in the city's history, Constantine adopted Christianity as the state religion of the Roman Empire and decided to build his new Christian capital in Byzantium, in sharp contrast to Rome (which was the centre of Paganism).

Named Constantinople and inaugurated in 330, Constantine's city was built on seven hills, like Rome. Constantine embellished his city with paved roads, splendid palaces, fountains, gigantic cisterns, churches and public baths, some of which still stand today. He adorned it with monuments taken from the four corners of the Roman Empire, including the Egyptian Obelisk which stands in the Hippodrome in front of the Blue Mosque.

Mosaic of Christ in the Kariye Camii

The founding of Constantinople as the new capital of the Roman Empire resulted in a shift of the imperial centre from Rome to the east and to the gradual assimilation of Roman Asia Minor into the Greco-Anatolian world. By the time Rome fell in 476, the assimilation was nearly complete. The Greek language of Anatolia eventually replaced Latin, and the remaining part of the Roman state came to be known as the Byzantine Empire.

Constantine's successor Valens (364–378) built giant aqueducts to transport water to the city from lakes north of Constantinople. Emperor Theodosius II (408–450) extended the city's land walls to their present boundaries, thus making the city almost impregnable. Emperor Anastasius (491–518) built periphery walls, stretching from the Black Sea to Çatalca, to bolster the city's outer defences after dangerous raids by Bulgarian and Slavic tribes.

The city became the cultural centre of the empire as many schools of religion and lay learning were established. The Council of Chalcedon in 451 raised the question of the relationship between the Church and state.

The Nika Revolt

In 532, Emperor Justinian imposed his iron-fist rule to suppress the anti-government Nika revolt, in which much of the city was destroyed in a fire and 30,000 people were killed. It was the worst bloodbath Istanbul has ever witnessed. Justinian reconstructed the city, rebuilding such edifices as Haghia Sophia, which had been burned down, and promulgated a code of laws for his land.

Over the next 900 years, Constantinople flourished as the biggest city in Europe and the Near East. It was a city of fabulous wealth and splendour at a time when London and Paris were squalid towns.

From 668 to 718, Arab armies laid siege to Constantinople several times and blockaded the city with their navies, but failed to crack the city's defences. Under Emperor Leo III, founder of the Isaurian Dynasty in the 8th century, Iconoclasm was adopted as a state policy. Images traditionally used in religious worship (icons), often great works of Church art, were smashed by religious zealots. Mosaics, frescoes, and illuminated manuscripts were destroyed in large quantities. In addition to image-breaking, the iconoclasts shut down monasteries and persecuted monks and nuns.

Except for a brief revival in the 9th century, this puritanical movement came to an end with the Church Council of Nicaea in 787, which restored the adoration of icons.

In the late 11th century, the Turks, a nomadic, warrior people who originated from the steppes of Central Asia, bearing the banner of Islam, thundered across the Anatolian hinterland in a campaign of conquest. In 1071, a Turkish army under Seljuk Sultan Alp Arslan routed a vastly superior Byzantine army and captured the Emperor Romanus IV Diogenes at Malazgirt (Manzikert), in eastern Anatolia. Suddenly the Byzantine Empire was threatened by the Muslim Turks. A series of Crusades over the next 370 years, sponsored by the Papacy seeking to unify the Catholic and Orthodox Christians, held back waves of Turkish horsemen.

In 1204, the Latin Crusaders turned their rapacious eyes on Constantinople, sacked the city and pillaged its wealth. They killed tens of thousands of Orthodox Christians, destroyed many magnificent buildings and carried off priceless relics to Venice. The bronze horses at St Mark's Cathedral in Venice were among the treasures removed. A Latin state was established in Constantinople, and the Byzantine Emperors fled to nearby Nicaea, modern day Iznik. Although the Byzantine Emperors recaptured Constantinople in 1261, the city never recovered from the plunder of the Crusaders, setting the stage for its conquest by the Ottoman Turks.

The Ottoman Turks

The Ottoman state had started out as a tiny principality under the Seljuk Turks in northeast Anatolia. Benefiting from the rivalries of other Turkish princes and weaknesses of the Byzantine state, the Ottomans unified the Turks in Anatolia and conquered the Balkans, surrounding Constantinople and the remaining territories of the Byzantine Empire with their grand armies.

On 29 May 1453, Ottoman Sultan Mehmed II conquered Con-

KURTULUŞ

İseppösü

Spor Caddesi

Şair Nedim Cad.

DOLMABAHÇE

Kadırgalar Geçidi

TAŞLIK
PARKI

University

Dolandere Cad.

Taşkışla

Cumhuriyet Caddesi

Taksim Caddesi

Direkçibaşı Sk.

Kurtuluş Sok.

TAKSİM

Dolabahçe Caddesi

Ömer Hayyam Cad.

TAKSİM

Dolmabahçe Sarayi
(Dolmabahçe Palace)

PAŞA

Dolapdere Cad.

University

Mete Cad.

- - - Ferry

Tarlabaşı

Caddesi

GALATASARAY

İnönü Cad.

KABATAŞ

Caddesi

Sahriye

TEPEBAŞI

Sıraselviler Cad.

Caddesi

Istiklâl Caddesi

Mebusan Yok.

Dolmabahçe
Camii

TEPEBAŞI
PARKI

İstiklâl Caddesi

Yeniçarşı Cad.

Kumrulu Yok.

Meclis-İMebusan Caddesi

lebi Cad.

BEYOĞLU

Bogazkesen Cad.

CİHANGİR

SİSHANE

Kumbaracı Yokuşu

Refik Saydam C.

İstiklâl Caddesi

Tersane Cad.

Okçu Musa C.

Voyvoda C.

Galata
Tower

Kemer Altı Caddesi

Necatibey Caddesi

Necatibey C.

Detterdar Yokuşu

Nusretiye
Camii

GALATA

Boğaziçi

KARAKÖY

(Bosphorus)

ÜSKÜDAR

Galata
Bridge

Galata Köprüsü

Leander's Tower
(Kız Kulesi)

MİNÖNÜ

aşa
mii

Yeni Camii
(New Mosque)

Hamidiye Cad.

Kennedy

Caddesi

Ankara C.

Mısır
Çarşısı

Sirkeci
Railway
Station

Zoo

Topkapi Sarayi
(Palace)

Cad.

Hoca Hanı S.

Harem

Sahil Yolu

Alemdar

Covered
Bazaar

Babali Cad.

GÜLHANE PARKI

Şeref Efendi S.

CAĞALOĞLU

Cad.

Mausoleums
of the Sultans

niçeriler Cad.

Divanyolu Cad.

ARŞIKAPI

Aya
Sofya
(Hagia Sophia)

Üçer S.

Sultanahmet
Camii

Caddesi

nanı Cad.

Özbekler S.

Kabasakal Cad.

Cankurtaran Ist.

SULTANAHMET

Cankurtaran Cad.

edy Caddesi

Küçük Aya
Sofya Camii

Kennedy

(Sea of Marmara)

Istanbul

500 m / 547 yards

Day Itineraries

Istanbul, one of the world's largest cities, is a vast metropolis stretching many kilometres in each direction. With more than 500 mosques, 150 churches and synagogues, a dozen palaces, ancient bazaars, and scores of public parks, it is one of the most colourful cities on this planet. But the main attractions of Istanbul are located in the European part of the city on the triangular peninsula that stands between the Golden Horn and the Sea of Marmara. This area comprises the Old City, which Turks call 'Stamboul'.

Visitors who want to make the best of a short stay are advised to try to find accommodation near Sultanahmet and Küçük Aya Sofya districts, which are within walking distance of most of the main touristic sights of the city. Many pleasant two- and three-star hotels, some of which are old mansions that have been renovated, can be found in this area.

The best way to tour Istanbul is to take long, leisurely walks,

The Blue Mosque

combined with taxi and *dolmuş* (shared taxi) rides. (Taxis and *dolmuş* are both plentiful and inexpensive.) If you find yourself succumbing to fatigue during your strolls, simply stop off for a short respite at one of the many outdoor coffeehouses that line the main touristic areas .

If you cross the Bosphorus, do as most Istanbulites do – take a ferry boat. A trip by ferry boat across the Bosphorus is not only relaxing, but also satisfying. You get a glorious vista of the city by sea, its many mosque minarets and churches romantically silhouetted against the skyline.

Avoid making the mistake of renting a car in the city. With traffic at a standstill most of the time, and parking spaces almost non-existent, driving in Istanbul is a nightmare and can easily ruin your precious vacation. If you do go ahead and rent a car, make sure it is chauffeur-driven.

Strolling in the Blue Mosque's courtyard

The Old City

Begin at Sultanahmet Park. Visit the Blue Mosque and the Carpets and Kilims Museum and then explore the ancient Hippodrome and the Turkish and Islamic Arts Museum. From there, visit the Sunken Palace and have lunch nearby. In the afternoon explore Hagia Sophia and the Turkish Handwoven Carpets Exhibition

Your first day in Istanbul will be spent getting acquainted with the city and its rich history. There is no better place to start a tour of Istanbul than Sultanahmet Park, the traditional political and religious hub of the city. The main sites are within walking distance and you can see them all during your first day.

You should get to Sultanahmet Park by 8.30am for a leisurely stroll of the district.

The Blue Mosque and the Sea of Marmara beyond

The northeastern end of the large park is dominated by Hagia Sophia, or Aya Sofya, a sixth-century Byzantine basilica turned mosque and now a museum. Sultanahmet Camii, better known in the west as the Blue Mosque, stands in the southwest corner. Only 180 metres (200 yards) separates the two holy buildings.

These two edifices dominate Istanbul's skyline with their piercing minarets and domes – one the highest achievement of the Christian world, the other the masterpiece of Islamic architecture. The scanty remains of the famous Hippodrome, where numerous chariot races were held during the Byzantine Period, are west of the park.

It was near this park that Byzas founded Istanbul 27 centuries ago. Constantine constructed his Great Palace where the park now stands. Justinian made several additions to the Great Palace in the fifth century, and its buildings spread down the hill from the present site of the Blue Mosque to the Sea of Marmara. You can still see traces of Justinian's palace behind the mosque and by the sea walls. During the Ottoman period, Sultanahmet Park was the religious centre of the city.

As the **Blue Mosque** is the earliest shrine to open its doors to the public, you will gain time by visiting it first. Like other mosques in the city, it is open seven days a week, from as early as 5.30am in summer and 6.30am in winter; it closes any time between 9 and 11pm.

The Blue Mosque is one of the most magnificent shrines in the Islamic world. It gets its name from the exquisite blue tiles that cover its interior walls. It has six minarets – a distinc-

Lights illuminate the Blue Mosque

tion at the time of its construction equalled only by El Haram, the mosque which surrounds the Kaaba in Mecca. The Blue Mosque was built by Ahmet I, who served as sultan from 1603 to 1618. Ahmet I was one of the two youngest sultans to rule the Ottoman Empire, ascending to the throne as a 12-year-old.

Like most imperial religious foundations, the Blue Mosque was the centrepiece of a complex of buildings, known as a *külliye*. In addition to the mosque, the complex included a *medrese* (higher Islamic institute of learning), a *türbe* (tomb of its founder), an *imaret* (public kitchens where food was served to the poor), a hospital, and a *caravansary* (where visiting traders and businessmen could stay) and a primary school. The hospital and *caravansary* were destroyed in a 19th-century conflagration. The public kitchens were located in the administration buildings of Marmara University, which stands at the southern end of the Hippodrome, before they, too, burnt down. Recently restored, the primary school stands above the northeastern entrance.

The *medrese* is located to the right of the northern precinct walls of the mosque and is used today to store some of the documents of the **Ottoman Archives**. Next to it is the **Tomb of Ahmet I** (9.30am–4.30pm, closed Monday and Tuesday), who was only 27 years old when he died. Buried next to him are his wife, Kösem Sultan, and his three sons, Osman II (sultan 1618–22), Murat IV (sultan 1623–40), Prince Beyazıt, and their relations. The sarcophagi are covered by dark green fabrics, symbolising the universality of Islam. Each sarcophagus of a male member has a turban-shaped tombstone, evoking images of life after death.

Kösem Sultan, one of the most powerful women ever to live in the Ottoman state, ruled the Harem and (historians suggest) the

Tombs of the sultans

Prayer beads

Empire, through her husband, two sons and grandson, Mehmet IV, for nearly five decades. The daughter of a Greek priest, she entered the harem at the very young age of 13 and won the heart of Sultan Ahmet with her beauty. Rival factions in the Harem, jealous of her influence over sultans, strangled her to death with a curtain cord in 1651.

Enter the mosque precinct through the northern gateway. The grounds of the Blue Mosque are vast. The ornate ramp you see to your immediate left leads to the Hünkâr Kasrı, a suite of rooms used by the sultan when he came here to pray. These lead into the Hünkâr Mahfili, the imperial quarters in the upper gallery of the mosque. The sultan usually attended the main Friday services, riding his white horse into the mosque precinct and up the ramp into his suite, which also had stables, giving the common people of Istanbul the opportunity to see him. Today the sultan's suite houses the **Carpets and Kilims Museum** (9.30am–12 noon and 1.30pm–4pm, closed Sunday and Monday), which has a remarkable collection of carpets and *kilims* from more than 200 mosques throughout Turkey.

Some of the carpets are several centuries old. The *kilims* are flat weaves, many of them collected from the various palaces.

The Blue Mosque is preceded on the western side by a large rectangular courtyard, or *avlu*, with a monumental gateway on each side. In its midst is an octogonal *şadırvan*, or fountain, where ritual washing once took place. Today, ritual washing, performed by Muslims before prayer, takes place at the taps along the northern exterior wall of the mosque.

From the courtyard, you can get a spectacular view of the cascading domes and half domes of the mosque. The main entrance to the mosque faces the courtyard, but this is usually reserved for Muslims coming to pray. Tourists are usually asked to enter through the northern door.

Blue Mosque interior

Faithful at prayer

You must remove your shoes when entering a mosque so as not to sully the carpets inside. Women must cover their hair, arms and legs with scarves. It is impolite to enter wearing shorts. To get an idea of what Islam is like, you could try to attend the main prayers at noon on Friday when 25,000 devout Muslims, wearing white skullcaps, cram its interior to bow down in supplication to Allah and listen to the *imam* (prayer leader) deliver his sermon.

With shafts of light penetrating its 260 windows, the mosque's interior conjures up images of heaven. Many of the windows are filled with stained glass, producing a kaleidoscope of colours. The walls are covered with 16th-century blue tiles that were produced in the kilns of Iznik, a city in western Anatolia which was famed for its ceramics. The interior is 51 metres (60 yards) by 53 metres (63 yards) and its 23-metre-high (80-ft-high) dome is supported by four 'elephant-feet' columns, and half domes.

Egyptian Obelisk

As you leave the Blue Mosque through the monumental gateway in the front courtyard, you come to **At Meydanı**, the ancient Hippodrome, which was the centre of civic affairs during the Byzantine era. In 203, Roman Emperor Septimius Severus began construction of the gigantic stadium, which was completed during the reign of Constantine the Great. In addition to providing public entertainment with its weekly chariot races and gladiatorial combats, it was a forum for the city's rival Greens and Blues factions, whose support the Emperor desperately needed to retain power. It was in the Hippodrome, in January 532, that Justinian's generals suppressed the Nika revolt, instigated by members of the two factions. Some 30,000 insurgents were slaughtered in a matter of hours.

Nothing remains of the stadium, except for three monuments in the middle of the Hippodrome, of which the **Egyptian Obelisk** or **Dikilitaş** is the most impressive. The Obelisk stands in the northern part of the Hippodrome. Commissioned by Pharaoh Thutmose III (1549–1503 BC) and erected originally at Deir el Bahri, opposite Thebes in upper Egypt, the 26-metre-high (84-ft-high) monument a rich collection of Islamic period relics and a wealth of ethnographic items, displaying every aspect of folk life of the nomadic Turks. One display shows how *kilims*, flat-weave carpets, are made. Another exhibits the various tents the Turks used while migrating to Anatolia from Central Asia in the 10th century, including the *karaçadırs*, *topakevs* and *yurts*. One panel display shows how various natural dyes, used in colouring carpets, are obtained. There are also exhibitions on Turkish village life and 19th-century Istanbul living. A pleasant, traditional, Ottoman-style coffeehouse on the ground floor serves tea and genuine Turkish coffee in a big garden that overlooks the Hippodrome.

Walk back to Sultanahmet Park. When you reach the end of Sultanahmet Park, cross the busy street known as **Divanyolu**, the **Council Avenue**, where many imperial parades were held during Ottoman times, to a small square on which you will see the **Bust of Halide Edip Adıvar**, a distinguished woman novelist who played a key role in the Turkish War of Independence (1919–22) with her fiery nationalistic speeches.

At the corner of the square is the entrance to one of the most remarkable sites of Istanbul, **Yerebatan Sarayı**, or the **Sunken Palace**. As you enter and walk down several flights of stairs, you will come to realise that it is not a palace at all, but a gigantic cistern, one of 18 built in the city during the Byzantine period as part of a huge interconnecting water network. It is sometimes also referred to as the **Basilica Cistern** (9am–6pm) because it is located diagonally across from Haghia Sophia. Constructed by Emperor Justinian the Great in the sixth century, Yerebatan Sarayı is 70 metres (77 yards) wide and 140 metres (155 yards) in length. A total of 336 columns, two of which have Medusa heads as bases, support its domes. The cistern was capable of holding as much as 80,000 cubic metres of water, sufficient to sustain part of the city during a long siege. Because of its vastness, Byzantine historians believed that a fleet of 16 warships could easily fit inside the cistern. Water was pumped to Yerebatan Sarayı from a reservoir near the Black Sea, 19 kilometres (12 miles) from Istanbul, by means of a series of aqueducts. The cistern still operates as water drips in constantly from the roof, and until recently you could actually rent a boat and row among the columns. A spectacular scene from the James Bond film, *From Russia With Love*, was staged inside the cistern. You can walk through the cistern along illuminated promenades, while listening to strains of Bach and Mozart.

Simit seller

Hagia Sophia

Two restaurants are located on the square above the cistern, The Sultan pub, specialising in Turkish cuisine, and Altin Kupa, which serves French and Italian dishes. Choose either of these for lunch.

Afterwards, cross Divanyolu and walk toward Haghia Sophia. Take a short detour along **Alemdar Caddesi** that runs along the western precinct of Haghia Sophia to **Caferağa Medresesi** (9am–7pm), a 16th-century theological school now serving as a handicraft centre. It is located in a cul-de-sac off this street. The rectangular *medrese* was constructed by Mimar Sinan (1497–1588), the most prolific Ottoman architect who ever lived. A contemporary of Michelangelo, Sinan served as chief architect from 1538 to 1588. According to Aptullah Kuran, an art historian, Sinan built 477 mosques, *medreses*, Turkish Baths and bridges, of which 319 are in Istanbul. You will see many of Sinan's works later during the day and during other tours of the city. At the handicraft centre, courses are given in traditional Turkish arts, including *hüsn-i hat* (calligraphy), *ebru* (which resembles batik), the making of meerschaum pipes, miniatures, stained glass, jewellery and carpets. Items made by specialists and students can be obtained from the centre, which also has a pleasant outdoor coffeehouse where you can rest before continuing to your next destination: Haghia Sophia.

Hagia Sophia, or **Aya Sofya** (open 9.30am–4.30pm), is the fourth largest cathedral in the world and the most magnificent Byzantine building ever constructed (St Paul's Cathedral in London, St Peter's in Rome, and Milan Cathedral are bigger). But Haghia Sophia was built centuries before the others, and it always stood out as a model for religious shrines. Ottoman architects, including Sinan, emulated it in their construction of imperial mosques, attempting to surpass it in magnificence, but were not always successful. The basilica, which served as the Patriarchal church during the Byzantine centuries,

From the outer narthex, you enter the immense interior, which covers an area of 1½ hectares (four acres). The first thing that strikes you about the interior is its ethereal, heavenly quality, dominated by its dome, which can be easily seen from every part of the church. Ancient historians felt its dome was suspended from heaven by a golden chain. Four gigantic piers support its dome that stands 56 metres (18ft) above the floor, which is about the height of a 15-storey building. The east-west diameter of the dome is 31 metres (102ft) and the north-south diameter is 33 metres (108ft).

The most fascinating mosaic in the nave has survived in the conch of the apse (the eastern side of the building). It depicts the Virgin Mary and the Christ-child on her knees. The child is dressed in gold, his right hand held out in blessing. In his left hand he holds a scroll. At the bottom of the arch which frames the apse is the colossal figure of the archangel Gabriel with his fluffy, bright-coloured feathers. On the north side of the arch, opposite the mosaic, you can see a few sad feathers of the archangel Michael. The other mosaics in the interior are located in niches at the base of the north tympanum wall, representing the three saints: St Ignatius the Younger; St John Chrysostom and St Ignatius Theophorus.

The only other mosaics in the interior are the famous six-winged seraphim or cherubim in the eastern pendentives. (Those in the western pendentives are imitations done by the Swiss Fossati brothers who were involved in the 1847–1849 restorations.)

The gigantic wooden medallions that were added by the Turks after the conquest are inscribed with the names of Allah, Mohammed, the first caliphs and the first two *imams* of the mosque. The Turks added a *mihrap*, a prayer niche, to the south side of the apse showing the direction of Mecca and a *minber*, or stepped pulpit from which the *imam* led the congregation in prayer. They also added the ornate sultan's box left of the apse.

You can find the remaining mosaics in the upper galleries, which can be reached by staircases opening into the outer narthex. Only one mosaic is in the northern gallery: it shows the Byzantine Emperor Alexander (912–13) in the full splendours of his ceremonial robe and crown of gold adorned with pearls. In the south gallery are several mosaics: one shows the famous Empress Zoe and her third husband, Constantine IX Monomachos. At the centre of the composition is Christ, his

Mosaic of Byzantine Emperor Alexan

Virgin Mary with the Infant Christ

right hand raised in a gesture of benediction. In his left hand he holds the Bible. To his left is the emperor offering a bag of money. The empress is to his right, holding a scroll. Married several times to weak sovereigns, Zoe ruled the empire from behind the scenes.

Another mosaic depicts the Virgin Mary holding the infant Christ. To her right stands the Emperor II Comnenus and to her left the emperor's wife, Eirene, holding a scroll. The last mosaic, known as the **Deesis**, is the fines. Although parts of the mosaic are lost, the features of the three figures are intact. In it, you can see Christ flanked by the Virgin and St John the Baptist, who are leaning toward Christ, seemingly pleading for the salvation of mankind.

Set into the pavement across from the Deesis is the **Tomb of Henricus Dandalo**, the Doge of Venice and one of the leaders of the Fourth Crusade. Dandalo was responsible for the sacking of Constantinople in 1204, when the Catholic Crusaders killed thousands of Orthodox Christians indiscriminately. Dandalo established a Latin kingdom in Constantinople, but he died in 1205. After the Byzantines recovered the city in 1261, according to Greek historians, mobs broke into the despot's tomb and tossed his bones to the dogs.

The last mosaic in Hagia Sophia stands over the vestibule door before the exit. It shows the enthroned Virgin Mary holding the Christ-child in her lap. On her right, Emperor Constantine the Great presents her a model of the city. Emperor Justinian offers her a model of Hagia Sophia.

Five Ottoman sultans and their families are buried in the precincts of Hagia Sophia, but the royal *türbes*, or mausoleums, are not open to visitors. The monarchs buried here include Mustafa I, who ruled briefly from 1617–18 and 1622–3, Deli Ibrahim, the mad sulta (ruled 1640–8), and Selim the Sot, the alcoholic son of Süleyman the Magnificent (ruled 1566–74). Selim died at the age of 54, after having fallen in his bath while in a fit of drunkenness. Besides Selim's catafalque is his favourite wife, Nurbanu, and the tombs of

Hagia Sophia mosaic

his five sons, three of his daughters and 32 children of his eldest son and successor, Murat III (1574–95). Upon Selim's death his other sons were murdered to allow the peaceful succession of Murat.

Murat's own *türbe* stands just beside his father. The night Murat died, 19 of his sons were killed to allow his eldest son, Mehmet III (1595–1603), to become sultan. This was the last time that fratricide was practised in determining the sultan.

When you leave Hagia Sophia, turn left and walk to the end of Sultanahmet Park. The building you see on your right is the **Haseki Sultan Hamamı**, a Turkish bath built by Sinan in 1556 in honour of Hürrem Sultan, wife of Süleyman the Magnificent. Now used as the **Turkish Handwoven Carpets Exhibition**, it is operated by the Culture Ministry. Inside reproductions of original motif carpets are on display and on sale. All the carpets are hand-made and coloured with root dyes. You might be able to get a bargain here as prices tend to be lower here than in private shops. In any case, the building itself is worth a brief tour.

Return to the entrance of the bath and walk straight along the eastern walls of Hagia Sophia. The structure you see on the right is the **Fountain of Ahmet III**, constructed in the early 18th century. To your left is the monumental back entrance to Hagia Sophia and Soğukçeşme Sokak, a narrow street between Hagia Sophia and the walls of Topkapı Palace lined with pastel-coloured houses. These 19th-century houses were in a state of dilapidation when they were taken over and renovated in the mid-1980s by Çelik Gülersoy, Turkey's best known promoter of art restoration, and his **Automobile and Touring Association**. Today the Touring Association operates them as the **Aya Sofya Pensions**, a pleasant series of hotels. Gülersoy has also turned a large cistern alongside the houses into a taverna-restaurant, known as the **Sarnıç**, or **Cistern Restaurant**, where excellent lunches and dinners are served. The Association also operates the **Istanbul Library** in the same street. With 6,000 volumes, it has the best collection of books on Istanbul in the world, and is open to scholarly research Mondays, Wednesday and Fridays. The Association has also opened the Konuk Evi, a new renovated hotel resembling the White House, across from the Istanbul Library. The hotel also has a fine, glass-enclosed restaurant and pub. Further down the street, on the left-hand side, is the Art Gallery, owned and operated by Ilhami Atalay and his artist family.

Return to your hotel for dinner and an early night after your first day in Istanbul.

Sogukçehme Sokak

Topkapı Palace

Tour of Topkapı Palace; lunch in the palace complex sitting on the terrace overlooking the sea; afternoon tea at Yeşil Ev; walk down to Küçük Aya Sofya Camii and Sokullu Mehmet Paşa Camii; visit the Armenian Church Patriarchate; dinner in Kumkapı.

You can spend a full day exploring **Topkapı Palace** (9.30am–4.30pm, closed Tuesday) and its various courts. But with a well-structured and organised visit you can see the most important sites within three or four hours, and even have lunch.

For almost 400 years, Topkapı Palace was the residence of the Ottoman sultans, the most powerful men in the world. The sultans sent shivers throughout Europe while their armies rushed from conquest to conquest. From within the walls of Topkapı Palace the sultans ruled a vast empire that stretched, in its heyday, from the gates of Vienna to the Indian Ocean and from North Africa to the Crimean Peninsula.

But the political intrigues and plots that were hatched in the Harem drove many sultans mad, led to the execution of many able statesmen and princes, and contributed to the slow decay and eventual collapse of the Ottoman Empire. In the 19th century, the palace came to symbolise the 'sick man of Europe'.

A city within a city, Topkapı Palace consists of interconnecting courts and groups of buildings and kiosks, re-

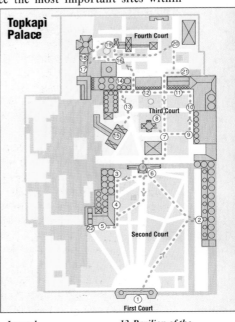

Legend:

1. *Gate of Salutations*
2. *Palace Kitchens*
3. *Armoury*
4. *Clock Room*
5. *Council Chamber*
6. *Gate of Felicity*
7. *Petition Room*
8. *Library of Ahmet III*
9. *Palace School*
10. *Treasury*
11. *Treasury*
12. *Manuscripts of Miniatures*
13. *Pavilion of the Sacred Relics*
14. *Chamber of the Mantle of the Prophet*
15. *Library and Mosque*
16. *Revan Kiosk*
17. *Circumcision Room*
18. *Baghdad Kiosk*
19. *Kiosk of Kara Mustafa Paşa*
20. *Mecidiye Pavilion (Konyalı Restaurant)*
21. *Sofu Camii*
22. *Harem*

flecting the feudal lifestyle of the nomadic Ottoman warriors. Anywhere
between 4,000 and 7,000 people
worked and lived inside it, serving
the imperial household.

Topkapı, which means Can-
non Gate, gets its name from
the two cannons that stood
by its sea walls. The Venetians, who fought against the
Ottomans for many centuries, described it as the Seraglio of the Grand
Signor. But to the Turks it was simply the Saray,
a Persian word adopted by them denoting a palace.

Topkapı Palace is located on the first hill of the old city,
encompassing the promontory known as **Saray Burnu** (Palace Point),
at the confluence of the Sea of Marmara, the Bosphorus and the
Golden Horn. Today, a modern highway and railway run along
the shore through parts of what were formerly the outer precincts
of the palace.

When Mehmet II conquered Istanbul in 1453, he built a palace
on the third hill of the city, where Istanbul University presently
stands. But he began constructing a bigger new palace, which became
Topkapı, to accommodate his growing retinue, and moved his residence there in the mid-1470s. The Old Palace, long gone, came
to be known as the Palace of Tears. To it were banished the harems
of deceased and deposed sultans and elderly palace servants, no
longer able to perform their duties. There they were separated from
the seat of power and forgotten.

Mahmut II (1808–39) was the last sultan to reside at Topkapı
Palace. Mahmut, who had a strong distaste for its bloody history,
moved to a new palace, the Dolmabahçe Palace, which he built
along the Bosphorus. The Topkapı thus became the Palace of Tears
where retired palace civil servants and ageing members of the Harem
were jettisoned. One of the last sultans, Abdülhamit II (1876–1909),
constructed a third palace at Yıldız, also along the Bosphorus,
where he took up residence. In 1924, one year after the proclamation
of the Turkish Republic and abolition of the sultanate, Topkapı
Palace was converted into a museum.

The main entrance to Topkapı Palace is through the **Imperial
Gate**, or **Bab-ı Hümayün**, opposite the northeastern corner of the
Fountain of Ahmet III. It leads to the **First Court**, also known as
the **Court of Janissaries**. Above the gate you can see the *tuğra*, or
emblem, of Mahmut II, the last sultan to have lived in the palace.
The inscriptions above the *tuğra* are of Mehmet II, the sultan who
conquered the city and built Topkapı. The Imperial Gate was always
open to the public, as it now is, but was guarded by sentries, who

would shut its massive doors only in times of anti-government disturbances. Sometimes, when riots occurred, these sentries connived with the mobs outside, allowing them to burst into the palace, seize an unpopular grand vizier or sultan, and execute him on the spot.

The long First Court is a public park lined with flowers and plane trees. During the Ottoman period state processions began and ended in this court, especially on Fridays when the sultan went to pray in one of the imperial mosques in the city. Today, tour group buses and taxis are usually parked inside. As you walk through the court, you will see **Hagia Eirene** or **Aya Irni**, the Church of Divine Peace, one of the oldest Christian shrines of Istanbul, to your left. It was constructed originally by Constantine the Great in the 4th century, serving as the Patriarchal cathedral until the completion of Hagia Sophia. The church burned down during the Nika revolt of 532, but was quickly rebuilt. When the Ottomans conquered the city, they turned it into an armoury. Hagia Eirene was restored during the Republican era and turned into a museum. Known for its superb acoustics, it is open now only for choral performances during the Istanbul Festival. The building next to it is the **Imperial Mint**, or **Darphane**, and it still operates, printing passports, official stamps and government documents.

At the very end of the court, just past the ticket booths, to your right, is the **Executioner's Fountain**, or **Cellat Çeşmesi**, where grand viziers (prime ministers) and other top political personages were beheaded on orders from the sultan. Executions were among the many duties of the palace gardeners. The heads of the executed officials were placed on columns in front of the fountain known as the **Warning Stone**, or **Ibret Taşı**, as grim reminders to others serving the sultan of what might befall them if they were to displease him. Although the risk of losing one's head was very high among top officials, especially grand viziers, this did not deter palace clerks from wanting influential positions, so attractive were the rewards. During the reign of Selim the Grim

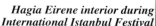
Hagia Eirene interior during International Istanbul Festival

(1512–20), so many grand viziers were beheaded that a favourite curse of the time was: 'May you be *sadrazam* to Sultan Selim.' (*Sadrazam* was the title of the grand vizier).

Entry to the **Second Court** is through the **Gate of Salutations** or **Bab-üs Selam**. Its two towers, resembling conical witches' hats, were used as dungeons to imprison candidates for the Executioner's Fountain.

Sixteenth-century miniature paintings depict gazelles grazing in the lawns of the spacious Second Court. Today the court is lined by cypress trees and flower gardens. To the immediate right are miniature models of Topkapı Palace as it was during the 16th century and as it is today. Take the lane that goes diagonally to the right. This leads to doors opening to the **Palace Kitchens**, a series of rooms now displaying the **Collection of Chinese, Japanese and European Porcelains**. In these chambers, food was cooked for between 7,000 and 20,000 people daily. A reproduction of the kitchens, with their huge cauldrons and other cooking utensils, can be seen in the room furthest to the northeast.

Two of the chambers show 4,584 pieces of Ming dynasty Chinese porcelain from a collection of more than 10,000 gathered by the sultans at various times. The celadon (special green-coloured dishes) were the most valuable in the collection because of their ability to change colour if poisoned food was placed on them. In the chambers across from the porcelain collections, you can see the **Silver and Crystal Collection**, of which the most interesting item is a miniature model of the Fountain of Ahmet III, done in silver and brass. The southernmost chambers house the **Topkapı Archives**, which has a good collection of original documents and manuscripts about the history of the early Ottoman Empire. The archives are open only to Ottoman researchers. The northernmost room contains the **Istanbul Porcelain and Glassware**, which came from a porcelain factory established by Abdül Hamit II on the grounds of Yıldız Palace. The collection of colourful glassware, known as the **Nightingale's Eyes (Çeşim-i Bülbül)**, is valued at several million dollars.

After viewing this part of the museum, re-enter the Second Court and cross over to the **Armoury**, in the northeastern corner. The Armoury has 400 weapons from various Islamic Empires, dating from the seventh century to the 20th century, including helmets, shields, swords, rifles, blunderbusses, armour and pistols, *tuğs* (horse-tails), which were emblems of rank. The most interesting item is the **Sword of Mehmet the Conqueror**, on which Islamic inscriptions are engraved in gold.

The enclosure with three domed rooms adjacent just south of the armoury is currently closed to visitors. It was in the **Council Chamber**, or **Divanhane**, where the grand vizier held periodic meetings with his *divan*, or cabinet, to determine government policies. Just above the chamber was the cubicle of the sultan, who could listen in on the proceedings through a latticed window. The sultan could interrupt meetings and express his view on decisions by banging his fist on the railings and barking commands through the open window. All government decisions needed the sultan's approval before they could become law. One of the domed rooms was reserved for the grand vizier. The others were secretariats where decisions were copied down in exquisite calligraphy. The room next to the armoury today houses the **Collection of Clocks** (closed to visitors). The **Tower of Justice** stands behind the Council Chamber and can be viewed from the court. This was used as a watch tower to observe the city, especially during civil upheavals that might threaten the palace.

The entrance to the Harem, where the palace women were sequestered, is through a door contiguous to the Council Chamber. Enquire at the ticket booth when the next guided tour will be given, and come back to it after viewing the rest of the palace and having lunch.

Southwest of the Harem, behind the walls, are the **Terrace and Quarters of the Halberdiers with Tresses (Zülfülü Baltacılar)**, who were named on account of the long locks of hair (*zülüfs*) that hung down from their headdresses along their cheeks. The halberdiers were Christian converts. Their duties were many. Once a month they carried wood into the Harem. They wore their collars turned up to shield their view of the females inside. This area, which also has a mosque and the **Display of Palace Coaches**, is closed to visitors.

From the Harem turn back and enter the **Third Court** through the **Gate of Felicity**, **Bab-üs Saadet**, which has an ornate roof, under which you can see 18th-century paintings of what appear to be palaces in

Harem, Topkapı Palace

the countryside. The Third and Fourth Courts together with the Harem were the realms of the Sultan. The moment you enter the Third Court you will see the **Petition Room**, or **Arz Odası**, where the sultan accepted foreign ambassadors and other visiting dignitaries. His throne, lined with rubies and pearls, stood at the back. The Petition Room is for the time being closed. Behind the Petition

Room lies the **Library of Ahmet III**, which resembles a mosque with a dome and raised portico. It is still used to house important palace manuscripts. A new library, on the western side of the court, is cleverly hidden by the wall. An odd-loking fountain, resembling a sundial, stands just to the northwest corner of the court in front of the Library of Ahmet III.

The buildings surrounding the court were part of the famous **Palace School**, where young Christian boys, taken from their families as a kind of tax levy and converted to Islam, were trained to become administrators of the empire. The most able youths rose to the ranks of grand vizier, *kaputan derya* (or grand admiral of the fleet), provincial governor or *beylerbeyi*, a supreme governor of an entire region of the empire. The young pages learned Arabic in order to read the Koran. They also learned to read and write the Ottoman script, based on Persian and Turkish languages, to ride horses and use bows. They also had to learn a trade, such as goldsmithing, basketweaving or calligraphy, which they might one day be forced to use should they fall from the sultan's favour and be expelled from the palace.

Now turn to your right and walk to the door opening in the wall to the **Display of the Sultans' Clothes**. At the present time only the childhood garments of Süleyman the Magnificent and the wardrobe of Mehmet II are on display.

The four chambers in the northeast corner of the Third Court hold the **Imperial Treasury**. Each room of the Treasury has a throne. Of these the **Throne of Ahmet III** is the most ornate. Inlaid with tortoiseshell and mother-of-pearl set with rubies and emeralds, it was used by Ahmet III, sultan 1703–33, on the eves of important religious holidays.

You can also see the 18th-century **Topkapı Dagger**, made from gold in which huge emeralds are set. The centrepiece of the Treasury is, indisputably, the **Spoonmaker's Diamond**, or **Kaşıkçı Elması**. Having 86 carats and embossed with 49 smaller diamonds, it is the fifth largest diamond in the world. It was this brilliant gem that

the character portrayed by the Greek actress Melina Mercouri attempted to steal in the film *Topkapı*.

The northernmost two-storey room houses the **Manuscripts of Miniatures and the Sultans' Portraits**. Turkish painting did not develop as fast as European art because the making of human images was forbidden by the Koran. The art form favoured by Ottoman painters was known as *husn-i hat*, or beautiful writing – calligraphy. But some of the court artists did miniature paintings, which they hid inside the pages of books, to avoid angering Islamic purists. The 16th-century miniatures you see in this chamber give a good picture of life under the sultans. They depict fleets battling, sultans bagging stags, military processions, janissary bands, acrobats, court jesters and belly dancers entertaining the sultan, amorous encounters, and half-naked women bathing in the Harem. Notice that Ottoman miniatures lack perspective.

One of the most interesting relics in this room is the remarkable **Map of Piri Reis**, showing the eastern half of the Americas. The map, made in 1513, was done on a piece of gazelle hide, based on Christopher Columbus's lost map. Piri Reis (1465–1555) was a prominent geographer and grand admiral of the fleet. His map confounds geographers even today because it was made only a decade after Columbus's voyages. At the time, it was still unclear that

Columbus had discovered a new continent. The upper gallery, housing the portraits of the sultans, is closed to the public.

The rooms in the northwest corner of the court are known as the **Pavilion of the Sacred Relics**. The chambers house objects associated with the Prophet Mohammed and other Muslim caliphs. According to Sabahattin Türkoğlu, former director of the palace, these relics were regarded as significant sources of 'spiritual and religious strength both by the state and ordinary people, rich and poor.' The articles were brought to Topkapı Palace after the Ottoman conquest of Egypt in 1517. The **Door of Repentance**, taken from the Holy Kaaba in Mecca, dominates the first room. The second room contains the footprint and a lock of hair be-

Gate of Felicity

Courtyard of the Valide Sultan

longing to Mohammed. The **Chamber of the Mantle of the Prophet** is closed, but can be seen through the latticed window. The mantle is kept inside a golden casket. You can also see Mohammed's sword.

The **Display of Embroideries** is in the room in the southwest corner of the Third Court. The embroideries, meticulously made by the women of the Harem, are inside the **Room of the White Eunuchs**, which housed the castrated white servants who were the sultan's personal guards.

You can enter the **Fourth Court** through the two passageways at the end of the Third Court to visit the numerous kiosks, or summerhouses, in its gardens. The left passageway takes you along a corridor of pillars to a water fountain, surrounded by three kiosks, overlooking Istanbul Harbour and the Golden Horn. These are the **Revan Kiosk**, the **Baghdad Pavilion** and the **Circumcision Room**, or **Sünnet Odası**. The Revan Kiosk was built in 1635 to celebrate the Ottoman capture of the Armenian city of Erivan (Revan) from Persia. The Baghdad Pavilion, a 17th-century structure, was used by the sultans as a reading room. The Circumcision Room got its name because young princes were circumcised in it, a practice that marked their entry into young adulthood.

The Fourth Court has three other summerhouses, the **Kiosk of Kara Mustafa Paşa**, an early 18th-century villa, the **Chamber of the Chief Physician** and the magnificent **Mecidiye Pavilion**, built by Abdul Mecit, sultan 1839–61, which he used to receive guests. The lower floor of the pavilion, which has a stunning patio overlooking the Sea of Marmara, has been operated for many years by **Konyalı Restaurant**, where you can have lunch before returning to the Harem. Konyalı, one of Turkey's oldest restaurant chains, has served many important statesmen in the past, including former

US President Richard Nixon, the late Shah of Iran, and Ethiopia's late Emperor Haile Selassie I. Although it has earned a good reputation by serving such eminent personalities, its prices are moderate. Try some of the lamb dishes that it specialises in, including *kuzu şaşlık*, tender morsels of lamb cooked on a skewer, as well as *meze* appetizers. After lunch, visit the tiny **Sofa Camii**, or Therace Mosque, just across from the Mecidiye Pavilion, before returning to the Second Court to see the Harem.

Although the **Harem**, or **Forbidden Place**, consists of more than 400 rooms, only a dozen are open to the public. Western sources have tended to view the Harem as virtually a private brothel of one man, the sultan. But, in fact, some sultans were monogamous and faithful to their wives. Others, including Deli Ibrahim, the 'mad sultan', were known womanisers. One sultan, Murat III, was officially credited with 103 off-spring from palace women. The Harem was a complete, self-sustaining unit, consisting of dormitories, private quarters, two small mosques, a school, a swimming pool and baths. Between 500 and 1,500 people lived within its walls, subject to strict discipline and a rigorous hierarchy.

Ottoman artistry

Other than the sultan, the only men permitted to enter the Harem daily were the black eunuchs, or *hadım ağas*, who formed the Harem's guard. These eunuchs were castrated Sudanese slaves, brought to Istanbul by Arab slave traders and sold to the palace. The chief eunuch, or Ağa of the House of Felicity, was below only the sultan, the grand vizier and the *seyhülislam* (minister of religious affairs) in rank. His special privileges and power were grounded in his access to the sultan and his ability to exploit rivalries between members of the Harem.

The most powerful woman in the Harem was the Valide Sultan, or mother of the ruling sultan. Under her were the wives, concubines and odalisques of the sultan, and servant women. The Valide Sultan had her own quarters and eunuchs, as did each wife and favoured

45

concubines. The children of the sultan, the potential heirs to the throne, lived in separate chambers.

Most of the women entered the palace either as war prisoners or as slaves, purchased through the Istanbul Slave Market. They were almost always Christians, but converted to Islam once in the palace. Many came from Caucasus, a region known for its beautiful women.

The Harem was a place of much intrigue and machinations. Power-hungry wives and concubines plotted the elimination of their rivals and their male children to allow their own sons to ascend the throne and permit them to become Valide Sultans. Beginning with the reign of Murat III (1574–95) and continuing for centuries, the women of the Harem asserted tremendous influence over the ruling sultans, the grand viziers and the affairs of state, in a period that came to be known as the Kadınlar Saltanatı, the Sultanate of Women.

You enter the Harem through the **Carriage Gate**. This brings you immediately to the **Guard Room** and the **Quarters of the Black Eunuchs**. The next gate, or **Cümle Kapısı**, opens to the **Golden Way**, a path of corridors and courtyards that runs from one end of the Harem to the other. You soon come to the **Quarters of the Valide Sultan**. It was here that Kösem Sultan ruled the empire through her husband, two sons and grandson and was strangled in 1651 on the orders of her daughter-in-law. Also murdered here in 1807 was Selim III, the most progressive sultan ever to reign, and his cousin and successor, Mahmut II, escaped assassination only by hiding in a cupboard. The next room you see is the **Sultan's Bath**, entirely furnished in marble and alabaster, followed by the **Room with Fountains**, with layered taps in the wall. Murat III used it as a bedroom and for conversations with his family. He would turn on the taps while discussing private matters to prevent servants

Room with Fountains

Fruit Room

from eavesdropping. The **Sultan's Chamber**, or **Hünkâr Sofası**, is the biggest room in the Harem. It was here that concubines entertained the sultan with belly dancing. The **Fruit Room**, or **Yemişli Oda**, nearby, had paintings of fruit on its walls to entice Ahmet III to eat. He was known to lack a strong appetite for food. The **Court of the Favourites** is surrounded by apartments, where each of the sultan's favourite concubines had rooms to herself.

The most interesting room in the Harem was the **Veliaht Dairesi**, the **Heir's Chambers**. After the abandonment of the practice of fratricide in determining the succession to the sultanate, all the heirs to the throne were held as virtual prisoners for years in this room to protect them from assassins and the intrigues of the Harem and ensure their eventual ascendancy. The throne always went to the eldest surviving male of the Ottoman dynasty. Often brother

succeeded brother, and the heir to the throne often spent most of his life in this chamber, also known as the **Altın Kafes**, or **Gilded Cage**. As a result, many young sultans were mentally unsuitable for their posts.

You leave the Harem through the Third Court. Return to the First Court and hail a taxi for your next destination – the **Green Mansion**, or **Yeşil Ev**, located at the eastern end of Sultanahmet Park behind the Haseki Sultan Hamamı. You can have late afternoon tea in the garden of Yeşil Ev, a 19th-century house that has been tastefully restored by Çelik Gülersoy and the Automobile and Touring Association and is now a moderately priced hotel. To one side of the hotel is a *türbe*, or tomb, of an old Muslim saint. The 18th-century **Medrese of Cedid Mehmet Efendi**, also renovated by the Touring Association and converted into the **Istanbul Arts Bazaar**, is to the other side. After resting, walk to the **Arasta** and the **Mosaic Museum** in **Kabasakal Sokak** (the **Street of the Bushy Beard**), behind the Blue Mosque.

The Arasta, a renovated shopping centre lined with gift shops, is part of the Blue Mosque Complex. The museum, a part of the Arasta, contains a good selection of late Roman period mosaics, discovered near the Blue Mosque.

After touring the Arasta and museum, walk down the hill 270 metres (300 yards) to **Kücük Aya Sofya Camii**, a former church transformed into a mosque. Built by Justinian in 527 as the **Church of Saints Sergius and Bacchus**, it is a tiny replica of Haghia Sophia. About 50 metres (55 yards) uphill to the north is the **Sokullu Mehmet Paşa Camii**, a mosque built by Mimar Sinan in 1571 for Esmahan Sultan, daughter of Selim the Sot and wife of Sokullu Mehmet Paşa, a Bosnian-born grand vizier who was assassinated in 1579. The mosque has the best 16th-century blue Iznik tiles in Turkey. Their unusual tulip motifs go up to the pendentives supporting the dome. Sokullu's mansion, just uphill, has been restored and is now operated as the **Sokullu Paşa Hotel** (Mehmetpaşa Sokak 10, Sultanahmet), one of the most charming hotels in this district.

From the hotel, follow the **Kadırga Liman Caddesi** to the district of **Kumkapı**, about 1km (½ mile) along some of the older, lower-middle-class neighbourhoods of the city. A run-down district along the Sea of Marmara, Kumkapı is full of charm. The district is renowned for its fish restaurants, churches and old houses. As

Kumkapı is located near the wholesale fish market, its restaurants serve the best fish in town. Kumkapı is also the Armenian quarter. A vast majority of Turkey's 70,000 Armenians are Gregorians who trace their conversion to Christianity to the year 301, a generation before Constantine the Great adopted it as the state religion of the Roman Empire.

You will be returning to the restaurant district, surrounding **Kumkapı Square**, for dinner. First though, spend half an hour or so touring the historical sites nearby before returning to Kumkapı Square. Visit the **Armenian Patriarchate** in Şarapnel Sokak (**Shrapnel Street**), off Kumkapı's main thoroughfare, **Kadırga Liman Caddesi**, several blocks west of Kumkapı Square. The Armenian Patriarch of Istanbul is subordinate to the Catholicos (Primate of the Armenian Church) at Echmiadzin, near Yerevan in Armenia. Across from the dilapidated building is the Patriarchate **Church of the Virgin Mary**, built in 1828, the principal Armenian shrine in Istanbul. Several Armenian Patriarchs are buried on its premises. The church is always open to the public. An Armenian high school is located along the same street.

The restaurants of Kumkapı are of the *meyhane* type, serving fish with an array of *meze* appetisers and *raki*, the national alcoholic beverage known as 'lion's milk'. The patrons of Kumkapı are generally local Turks, intellectuals, journalists and foreign tour groups. Several celebrated foreigners have dined here, including Mikis Theodorakis, the renowned Greek Communist politician and composer famed for his musical score of the film *Zorba the Greek*. Several of the restaurants are also Armenian-owned, including the **Kör Agop** – the Blind Agop, so-called because the propritor was sightless in one eye (Ördekli Bakkal Sokak No 7) – one of the most venerated establishments in this seedy district. It specialises in *karides güvec*, a shrimp casserole, and *kırlangıç,* a tasty broiled tub fish in a frothy lemon base and served in a ceramic cauldron. Another good eatery is **Fırat Restaurant** (Çakmataş Sok 11/A), which serves delightful *kalamar*, or fried

Fish auction at the fish market

squid. **Üçler Balik Restaurant** (Ördekli Bakkal Sok No 7), operated by an Albanian Turk, is probably the best. Try some *pavurya*, crab meat served as a *meze,* which is their speciality. Those who dislike fish can order *biftek*, a kind of sandwich steak, or *arnavut ciğeri*, a tasty fried liver served with *pilâv*, a rice dish. Evenings can get crowded and boisterous. Fiddlers sometimes come and sit at tables to play gypsy airs while women performers sing sad songs of old Istanbul for a modest fee.

Along the Bosphorus

Enjoy a ferry boat ride, take a walk up the Anadolu Kavağı Fortress to view the Clashing Rocks and the Black Sea; visit the many palaces and don't forget a stroll through Yıldız Parkı, Istanbul's greatest park.

Day three is spent touring the **Bosphorus** by ferry boat and by car. Special tour ferry boats leave three times a day from the **Bosphorus Ferry Boat Landing (Boğaz Vapurları Iskelesi)** in Eminönü, at the foot of the Galata Bridge. The two-way trip costs about US$6. The tour boat is usually very crowded in the summer, but it is nonetheless an enjoyable journey. Take the morning boat. As it does not leave until 10.30am, do some shopping around the Sirkeci and Eminönü business districts, or walk along the Galata Bridge for a good view of the harbour before boarding. You will be getting off at the last village, Anadolu Kavağı for lunch. Sit out on the deck to get the best view of Istanbul.

A narrow, twisting waterway that severs Europe and Asia and connects the Black Sea with the Sea of Marmara, the Bosphorus is 30 km (19 miles) in length, ballooning from a waist of 760 metres (831 yards) to 3km (2 miles). A number of towns, villages and tiny settlements cling to its scenic shores lined with 19th-century palaces,

Legend:
1 *Galata Bridge*
2 *Leander's Tower*
3 *Mimar Sinan University*
4 *Çirağan Palace*
5 *Ortaköy*
6 *Galatasaray Island*
7 *Bosphorus Bridge*
8 *Beylerbeyi Palace*
9 *Sadullah Paşa Yalısı*
10 *Kuleli Military High School*
11 *Robert College*
12 *Bosphorus University*
13 *Kandilli Observatory*
14 *Palace of Küçüksu*
15 *Rumeli Hisarı*
16 *Anadolu Hisarı*
17 *Fatih Bridge*
18 *Köprülü Amcazade*
    Hüseyin Paşa Mansion
19 *Khedive's Palace*
20 *Paşabahçe Glass Factory*
21 *Büyük Tarabya Hotel*
22 *Anadolu Kavağı*
23 *Symplegades (Clashing Rocks)*
24 *Tomb of Telli Baba*
25 *Sadberk Hanım Museum*
26 *Summer Residence of German*
    Embassy
27 *Presidential Summer Palace*
28 *Emirgân Park*
29 *Mansions of Damat Mehmet*
    Ferit Paşa
30 *Yıldız Parkı*
31 *Mausoleum of*
    Barbarossa Hayrettin
32 *Naval Museum*
33 *Ilyas Restaurant*

old wooden houses known as *yalìs*, and magnificent modern mansions.

The Bosphorus gets its name from an amorous affair that Zeus, the chief god of the Olympic pantheon, was having with the gorgeous goddess Io. According to the myth, Zeus's jealous wife, Hera, sent a swarm of flying gnats to irritate Io. The goddess turned herself into a heifer, plunged into the waterway from the Asian shore, and swam across to escape the gnats. Thus the waterway was called the Bosphorus, or the 'Ford of the Cow'.

The next mythical event associated with the Bosphorus was the passage of Jason and the Argonauts on their way to seek the recovery

The busy, busy Bosphorus

of the Golden Fleece from the land of the Colchis, at the eastern end of the Black Sea.

There are two currents in the Bosphorus: the predominant surface current runs from the Black Sea to the Sea of Marmara. A stronger subsurface current at a depth of 40 metres (144ft) runs in the opposite direction. If one wished to sail up the Bosphorus to the Black Sea without using a motor, one would have to drag a heavy anchor or a fish net to catch the lower current, as was the practice in ancient times.

Shaped like an S, the Bosphorus is one of the busiest waterways in the world. Hundreds of giant oil tankers and super cargo ships pass through it daily. Turkish maritime authorities strongly recommend foreign ships to take pilots when navigating the waterway. In addition to the foreign flag ships, naval vessels and Turkish cargo boats that cross it, the Bosphorus is usually congested by a host of smaller craft: commuter ferry boats plying between the two banks, little coasters and fishing boats clogging the route. The passage has always been dangerous to shipping because of its erratic currents and the thick fog which descends without warning, reducing visibility to zero. Some winters, icebergs float down from the Black Sea, cluttering the channel and closing it to traffic.

The Bosphorus has always been coveted by the Black Sea nations, particularly Russia, because it is their only outlet to the warm waters of the Mediterranean. Tsarist Russia fought many wars for the control of this strategic body of water. Even the Cold War began because of Stalin's demands for joint Soviet bases on the Bosphorus. By controlling the passage, the Turks, in the words of Winston Churchill, 'pinch Russia's nostrils'. Each year hundreds of warships of Russia and the Ukraine pass through, travelling from naval bases on the Crimean Peninsula to the Middle East. If you are lucky during your boat ride, you may see some Russian warships, including the stupendous aircraft carrier *Kiev*, as they navigate the straits.

Once the boat leaves dock, you quickly pass **Saray Burnu** with **Topkapı Palace** on your right. To your left is **Karaköy** and the main port facilities, with scores of visiting Turkish, Greek and Russian ocean liners tied to the pier. You can see the silhouettes of Istanbul's biggest hotels, the **Swiss**, the **Etap Marmara** and the **Hilton** in the hills. To your right is the Sea of Marmara and the beginning of the Asian shore of Istanbul. During the next three days of excursions, you will come back and visit many of the sites you pass by boat today.

Your boat soon glides by **Leander's Tower** (Kız Kulesi), a light-house built originally as a defensive watch tower by Athenian states-man Alcibiades. It was reconstructed as a lighthouse in the 12th century by Byzantine Emperor Manuel I Comnenus and dedicated to the legendary Leander, who drowned while swimming across to his loved one, the Priestess Hero. The lighthouse marks the beginning of the Bosphorus. To your left is **Mimar Sinan University**, a fine arts college named after the famous 16th-century Turkish architect, and the ornate **Dolmabahçe Palace**, a latter-day residence of the

Fisherfolk

Ortaköy Mosque

sultans. Behind it is **Inönü Stadium**, named after Turkey's second president, Ismet Inönü. To your right is **Üsküdar**, an old pious part of the city filled with many fine mosques.

Your captain soon stops at **Beşiktaş**, one of Istanbul's most populous districts, to take on more passengers. The boat pushes on, passing the newly restored **Çırağan Palace**, which has become a plush hotel and convention centre operated by a German company, on the European side. Before it burned down in 1910, it was used as the Parliament Building after the 1908 revolution of the Young Turks. **Ortaköy**, or **Middle Village** – so-called because it is supposedly at the midway mark of the Bosphorus – has a fine 19th-century mosque standing next to the **Bosphorus Bridge**. Built in 1973, this is the fifth-longest suspension bridge in the world and the second-longest in Istanbul. The 1,074-metre (3,525-ft) Bosphorus Bridge is 7 metres (25ft) longer than the George Washington that spans the Hudson in New York. But it is shorter than the Verrazano-Narrows Bridge, New York (1,298 metres/4,260ft); the Golden Gate Bridge, San Francisco (1,280 metres/4,200ft); the Fatih Bridge, Istanbul (1,190 metres/3905ft); and the Mackinac Bridge, Michigan (1,158 metres or 3,800ft).

Across on the Asian side, you can see the **Beylerbeyi Palace**, by

the bridge's huge pier. The palace, constructed in 1865 by Sarkis Balyan, a member of the famous 19th-century Armenian family of architects, served as a summer lodge for foreign dignitaries, including Britain's King Edward VIII and Emperor Franz Josef of Austria.

Scenic city on the shore

Next you pass **Galatasaray Adası**, a tiny island owned by sports club Galatasaray. A favourite summer hang-out for Istanbul businessmen, it has a swimming pool, a restaurant and game rooms. To your right is **Çengelköy**, the **Village of Hooks**, so-called because after the Turkish conquest anchor hooks were discovered there. **Sadullah Paşa Yalısı**, a 19th-century dark red-coloured mansion nearby, is owned by Ayşegül Nadir, the scandalous ex-wife of the fugitive Turkish Cypriot tycoon Asil Nadir. The Nadirs have, in better days, hosted Britain's Princess Margaret and other members of the British royal family here. The mansion gets its name from Sadullah Paşa, an Ottoman diplomat who was one of its previous owners. Nearby is **Kuleli Kışlası**, a military barracks with towers built in 1828 and now serving as the **Military High School**.

Bosphorus dwellings

The next village on your left is **Arnavutköy**, or the **Albanian Village**, which has numerous Greek churches and pleasant seafood restaurants. On a hill overlooking the town is **Robert College**, an American co-educational high school originally established by US missionaries in 1871 as the **American College for Girls**. The girls' college and the men's lycée, Robert College, which was located in Bosphorus suburb, Bebek, merged in 1971.

Turning at the hook known as **Akıntı Burnu** (Cape of Currents), the deepest part of the Bosphorus, one comes to Bebek, a fashionable district where wealthy businessmen, glamorous movie stars and foreign dignitaries reside. On the hill stands the buildings of Bosphorus University, one of Turkey's leading schools of higher education. It was established in 1971 on the grounds of old Robert College.

If you look to the Asian side, you will see the township of **Kandilli**, famed for the **Kandilli Observatory**, which was established in 1911. You can also see the **Count Ostorog Yalısı**, a seaside mansion built by Count Ostorog, a French nobleman of Polish descent who served in

Lighting up the Bosphorus

high position in the Ottoman court in the early 1900s. Nearby is the village of **Küçüksu**, which has one of Istanbul's best known public parks and the **Palace of Küçüksu**. Constructed for Sultan Abdül Mecit in 1857 by Nikogos Balyan, a member of the illustrious Armenian family of architects, the palace is now a museum. Nearby is the **Kıbrıslı Mustafa Emin Pasa Yalısı**, built in 1760, the largest wooden mansion on the Bosphorus with a facade measuring 60 metres (66 yards) in length.

The boat now zips past the two castles known as the 'Cut Throats' (Boğaz Kesen), which stand opposite each other, **Rumeli Hisarı** on the European side and the smaller **Anadolu Hisarı** on the Asian side of the straits. Built by the Turks before the conquest, they were aimed at cutting off aid to the besieged city from the Black Sea. You will visit Rumeli Hisarı later in the day. The fortresses stand at the narrowest point of the waterway. It was here that the Persian King Darius built a bridge of boats in 512 BC to transport his huge army in a campaign against the Scythians.

You next pass **Fatih Bridge**, the third-longest suspension bridge in the world. Built in 1987 by a Japanese-Turkish consortium, led by C Itoh Corporation, it is the second crossing spanning the Bosphorus. The bridge is named after Fatih Sultan Mehmet (Mehmet II), the conqueror of Istanbul. The dilapidated red mansion you see along the shore is the **Köprülü Amcazade Hüseyin Paşa Yalısı**, built in the late 17th century by the grand vizier Köprülü Amcazade Hüseyin Paşa.

The boat then stops off at **Kanlıca**, a picturesque village on the Asian shore with quaint seaside fish restaurants and coffeehouses. The village is known for its delicious yogurt, served with a heaped spoon of sugar. Across on the European side you can see the village of **Emirgân**, famous for its immense park with tulip gardens.

Gliding by Rumeli Hisarı

From Kandili, the boat hugs the Asian shore, passing the villages of **Çubuklu**, **Pasabahçe** and **Beykoz**. The **Palace of the Khedive**, or **Hidiv Kasrı**, dominates the hill overlooking Çubuklu with its rococo architecture and twin spires and public park, operated by the Automobile and Touring Association of Turkey. The sprawling complex by the shore is the **Department of Navigation, Hydrography and Oceanography**. At Paşabahçe, you can see the smokestacks of **Paşabahçe Cam Fabrikası**, one of the biggest glass manufacturers in the world. Beykoz is a town of fishermen and public parks. Across on the European side are the villages of **Yeniköy** and **Tarabya**. Yeniköy has many pleasant seaside mansions. Tarabya is famous for its many fish restaurants and the round **Büyük Tarabya Hotel**, the best hotel on the Bosphorus.

The Bosphorus veers sharply to the left after Tarabya and enters **Büyükdere Koyu**, the Bay of Büyükdere where its girth widens to 3km (2 miles). The boat stops off at **Sarıyer**, a large township on the European shore, and then it proceeds to **Rumeli Kavağı**, a pleasant fishermen's village with many fishing boats tied up at the

wharf. You can see the mouth of the Black Sea from here.

The boat next crosses to Asia and comes to its last halt, **Anadolu Kavağı**, where your boat will dock for the next two or three hours. This will give you the opportunity to have lunch and explore the village, famed for its fish restaurants that serve modestly priced seafood. Choose any of Anadolu Kavağı's restaurants for a sumptuous meal of fried *kalkan* (turbot) or grilled *lüfer* (blue fish), with appetisers such as *midye tava* (fried mussels), *zeytinyağlı barbunya* (beans served in olive oil), and *haydari*, a delicious yogurt dip served mixed with garlic and parsley.

Anadolu Kavağı, you will quickly note, is a military zone. After lunch walk up the hill to the **Genoese Fortress** on top of

Küçüksu Palace

Beylerbeyi

Atatürk, founder of the Turkish republic, is usually docked by the quayside in Istinye.

In the next town, Emirgân, take a quick tour of the delightful **Emirgân Park**, renovated and operated by the Automobile and Touring Association. The park has three pavilions, the **Pink Kiosk**, the **Yellow Chalet**, where refreshments are served, and the **White Pavilion**, where classical music performances are now given. During the Ottoman Period the park was owned by the Khedives of Egypt (the Khedive was the title given to the Turkish viceroys of Egypt 1867–1914) who built the pavilions. The best time to visit Emirgân is during spring when red, yellow and blue tulips blanket the park. Tulip growing originated in the private parks along the Bosphorus among Ottoman notables of the early 18th century in emulation of Western ways. Emirgân has several pleasant coffeehouses on its main square under a plane tree, facing the Bosphorus. There you can see many starry-eyed men ensconced in wooden chairs, smoking *nargiles* and watching ships sail by.

Balta Liman, the next town, is famous for the **Büyük Reşit Paşa**

Tulips in full bloom

Yalısı, a 19th-century mansion which today is used as the **Balta Liman Orthopedics Hospital**. It was constructed by Büyük Reşat Paşa, the grand vizier who was responsible for the westernising Tanzimat reforms of 1839. The enclosed area immediately behind the hospital is the **Mansion of Damat Mehmet Ferit Paşa** (1853–1923), one of the last grand viziers of the Ottoman Empire. The mansion and its support buildings together serve as the **Social Centre of Istanbul University**.

When you reach the town of **Rumeli Hisarı**, visit the enormous fortification by the same name that dominates the European shore of the Bosphorus. Rumeli Hisarı (9.30am–5pm, closed Monday) was constructed by Mehmet II in 1452, one year before his conquest of Constantinople. The castle is 250 metres (273 yards) in length and 125 metres (137 yards) at its broadest point. Spanning a deep valley, it has two tall towers on the opposite hills and one at the bottom of the valley by the shoreline. During the Istanbul Festival, the castle is used to stage famous plays, including Shakespeare's *Hamlet*, *Macbeth* and *Othello*.

Return to your taxi and drive to Bebek and Arnavutköy. The grey massive building you see on your left is the **Egyptian Consulate**, built during the 19th century by the Khedives of Egypt. Arnavutköy has many old wooden houses, now in a sad state of dilapidation, clinging to the hillside, and a half dozen Orthodox churches, including **Ayi Strati Araksiarhi**, an impressive building near the post office.

From Arnavutköy continue past the villages of **Kuruçeşme**

View from the top

Castle at Rumeli Hisarı

and **Ortaköy** and come to the enchanting **Yıldız Parkı**, the biggest public park in Istanbul, where you can have late afternoon tea. Have your chauffeur drive you to the very top of the park so you can tour its two pavilions and two *serras*, or winter coffeehouses. The park was part of **Yıldız Palace**, a latter-day residence of the Ottoman sultans that lies just northwest of the grounds. At Yıldız, you can admire the creations of the tragic Abdülhamid II, the last of the great sultans who became, amid the self-imposed solitude of his palace, one of the most accomplished carpenters of his empire. Take time to appreciate the perfectly reproduced Viennese and Swiss cafés in the vast park surrounding the palace which once served him (their only customer). In 1979, the Automobile and Touring Association renovated the park and buildings, turning Yıldız Parkı from a neglected wilderness into a well-kept palace garden. The association operates the buildings as restaurants, coffeehouses and delicatessens.

The brick-red-coloured **Çadır** (Tent) **Pavilion**, which overlooks a large pool of goldfish, was the site where Ahmet Şefik Mithat Paşa (1822–84), the grand vizier responsible for preparing the Ottoman Empire's first constitution in 1878, establishing the first National Assembly, was tried on trumped-up charges of murdering

Abdül Aziz (sultan 1861–76). Found guilty, he was exiled to Yemen where he was executed.

Resembling a pink mushroom, the **Pink Serra**, or **Winter Garden**, serves as a fancy pastry shop in winter. Everything inside is pink and white. The floor is in pink marble, while the antique plates and decanters arranged in the showcases are wine-coloured. The **Green Serra**, another patisserie, is located under high trees in a valley just beyond the Pink Serra. This winter garden is decorated with green tables, chairs and lanterns, harmonising with the surroundings. During the reign of Sultan Abdülhamit, the **Malta Kiosk** was used for official receptions. The kiosk has a pleasant courtyard, surrounded by blossoming Judas trees and bougainvillea. Have your taxi wait while you have tea.

After visiting Yıldız Parkı return to the main avenue running along the Bosphorus and drop by the Giragan Palace, now a hotel, restaurant and convention centre run by Kempinski Hotels of Germany. The Palace itself served as the new Turkish Parliament after the constitution of 1908. The interior has been delightfully restored with pastel colours and crystal bannisters.

In the next town, Beşiktaş, visit the **Mausoleum of Barbarossa Hayrettin** (1466–1546), the Ottoman grand admiral whose navies turned the Mediterranean into a Turkish lake in the 16th century. Just behind the mausoleum, in the park, you can see the **Statue of Barbarossa Hayrettin**. Six verses written by the poet Yahya Kemal Beyatlı (1884–1958) are inscribed on the southern side of the pedestal. They roughly translates as:

Malta Kiosk

Whence on the sea's horizons comes that roar?
Can it be Barbarossa now returning
From Tunis or Algiers or from the Isles?
Two hundred vessels ride upon the waves.
Coming from lands the rising Crescent lights:
O blessed ships, from what seas are ye come?

If the **Naval Museum** (Deniz Müzesi), located behind the statue, is still open when you get there, visit it. The museum is open every day, except Mondays and Tuesdays, from 9 am to 5 pm. The two-storey museum has a good collection of artifacts from various naval engagements fought by the Turks over the centuries. These include battles against the Venetians in the 16th century, the Dardanelles campaign of 1915 against the British and French, and the 1974 Cyprus conflict fought against the Greeks and Greek Cypriots. Its garden is littered with naval artillery pieces, anchors and propellers of famous Turkish warships. A mural map of the Ottoman Empire at its zenith is displayed in its wall. One of the most interesting items in the garden is the wreck of a German U-boat that hit a mine and sank off the Black Sea mouth of the Bosphorus during World War I. The wreckage was discovered in 1993 by miners digging for coal in an area that had been reclaimed from the sea. Another part of the museum which faces the **Hayrettin Iskelesi**, or **Hayrettin Boat Landing**, displays the **Sultans' Galleys** (Padişah Kayıkları),which the sultans used for outings with their harems.

For dinner drive to **Nişantaşı**, a modern neighbourhood with chic clothes shops and fancy restaurants up in the hills of the new city. This is the most fashionable residential area in the city proper, where you can study Turkish fashion – both male and female – at its most ostentatious. To get there your taxi will pas **Akaretler**, a series of old interconnected buildings that are being turned into a five-star hotel, and the **Maçka Maden Fakültesi**, Istanbul Technical University's **Faculty of Mining and Mineral Engineering**, an impressive palatial building. You will also pass the four-star **Maçka Hotel**. The district gets its name from the monument (Nişantaşı) at the corner of **Rumeli Caddesi**, commemorating the reign of Sultan Mahmut II.

Get off at the monument and turn left at Rumeli Caddesi and cross the street. Enter the passageway with **Ilyas Restaurant** written on its exterior and walk down steps to the basement. Ilyas Restaurant resembles a subway station. Several tables and the kitchen are located in what looks like a train. Ilyas is famous for its grilled meats (*karışık ızgara*) and vegetable dishes. It has live Western music in the evenings.

The New Turkey

A Tour of the New City

Step into the dark Underground Mosque; join a tour of the magnificent Dolmabahçe Palace. Take a tram ride; enjoy a drink at the Flower Passage and watch the world pass you by. Refresh yourself with an invigorating rub-down at the Turkish baths.

Your fourth day will be spent touring the district of **Karaköy**, the lower Bosphorus, Taksim Square and Beyoğlu. This part of Istanbul was known as **Galata**, after the Celts (or Gauls) who once besieged the city during Roman times, and **Pera**, which in Greek meant

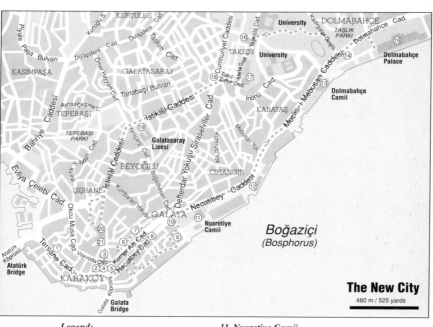

The New City

480 m / 525 yards

Legend:
1   Arap Camii
2   Tünel
3   Podestat
4   Karaköy Square
5   Yeralti Camii)
6   Church of St Benoit
7   Church of St Gregory
8   Turkish Orthodox Patriachate
9   Istanbul Stock Exchange
10 Kılıç Ali Paşa Camii

11 Nusretiye Camii
12 Mimar Sinan University
13 Dolmabahçe Camii
14 Clock Tower
15 Dolmabahçe Palace
16 Sheraton Hotel
17 Atatürk Cultural Centre
18 Taksim Square
19 Galatasaray Square
20 Galata Tower
21 Giraffe Street

'beyond'. It was the district that stood beyond the Old City, Stamboul, across the Golden Horn. But to the Muslim Ottoman Turks it was simply called **Giavur Şehiri**, the City of the Infidel, because it was almost entirely inhabited by Christian Greeks, Armenians, Venetians, Genoese, British and Jews, carrying out trade from immense buildings and residing in splendid stone houses, many of which can still be seen today.

In the words of Edwin A. Grosvenor, an American historian who lived in Istanbul in the late 19th century, Pera was a 'Western city stranded in the East, a European metropolis, making part and parcel of the Mussulman [Muslim] capital, and yet seeming in its Occidental life and customs a protest against an Asiatic civilisation and creed.' The languages spoken in Pera were mainly French, Italian and Greek. In its 19th-century heyday, the district had hundreds of high-class dance halls, tavernas and cabarets, where European women entertainers performed the can-can and alcohol flowed freely. It was a part of the city avoided and shunned by the pious Turks who looked disapprovingly upon its gay nightlife. The sumptuous embassies, which were downgraded to consulates after the Turkish capital was moved to Ankara in 1923, still line **Istiklâl Caddesi**, or the **Grand Rue de Pera**. But the back streets of Pera and Galata are now virtual slums. The wealthy Christian inhabitants have all but disappeared, to be replaced by Turkish peasant migrants.

Smoking hubble bubble at Galata Bridge

The district acquired its present form under the Genoese. After the Byzantine Emperors reconquered Constantinople from the Latins in 1261, they granted the district as a semi--autonomous colony to the Genoese. The district was ruled by a *podesta*, or governor, appointed by Genoa. The Genoese fortified their town, constructing protective walls around it. After the conquest, the Turks removed the walls, but the district became the European quarter of Constantinople.

Most of the shrines you will see in the area are Christian churches, many of them still in use. The mosques were primarily built along

Taxi anyone?

the shore on land that had been reclaimed from the Bosphorus and filled in. Many of these were erected in the 19th century and have baroque and rococo architectural styles, displaying the preference of their Christian architects and the strong influence of the West on late Islamic art.

Begin your tour of Karaköy at **Arap Camii** around 9am. Arap Camii, located on a side street just off **Tersane Caddesi** (Shipyards Street), is a 14th-century Latin church converted by the Turks into a mosque. The campanile is now used as a minaret from which the *imam* (prayer leader) calls the faithful to prayer five times a day. The cross at the top belfry has been replaced by an Islamic crescent. The Turks added the ablutions fountain.

Walk to Tersane Caddesi and turn north in the direction of the Bosphorus. This area, called **Perşembe Pazarı**, or the **Thursday Bazaar**, is the principal market for imported and locally produced hardware, sold among the many shops lining Tersane Caddesi. You then pass the **Tünel**, a two-stop, 550-metre-long (1,804-ft-long) subway that was built in 1874 to connect Karaköy with Beyoğlu. Until summer 1989, this was Istanbul's only underground.

Walking along, you come to **Karaköy Square**, a busy intersection. To your right is the Galata Bridge and the Golden Horn. To your left is **Yüksek Kaldırım**, a steep paved street that leads to Beyoğlu. The building with a tower-like crown standing at the corner of Yüksek Kaldırım and **Bankalar Caddesi** (Avenue of the Banks) was the ancient **Podestat**, the **Palace of the Genoese Governor of Pera**.

At Karaköy Square take the underpass to the other side of the intersection. If you take the side street that runs between **Necatibey Caddesi** and **Rıhtım Caddesi**, you will come to one of the most astonishing sites in Istanbul – the **Underground Mosque** (**Yeraltı Camii**). This odd mosque, located in the basement of a building, once stood at the lower depths of the Genoese walls that surrounded this part of Istanbul. It is more like a gloomy dungeon than a place of worship.

If you continue along this street you come to the **Port of Istanbul**. To your right are the **Karaköy Vapur skelesi**, the ferry boat landing, and the **Deniz Otobüsü Iskelesi**, the Sea Bus landing. Big foreign cruise ships dock along the pier straight ahead. Turn left here, take the first right and left

Flying the flag

Atatürk's Room, Dolmabahçe Palace

Nikogos Balyan, who collaborated with his father, Karabet. The sultans borrowed heavily from foreign banks and emptied the state coffers to build the lavish 600-metre-long (656-yard-long) palace, which surpasses its European counterparts in magnificence and opulence. Dolmabahçe Palace served as the principal imperial residence until later sultans, mainly Abdül Hamit, moved to Yıldız Palace on the hill above Beşiktaş. During the last years of the empire, it was used solely for ceremonial purposes and for the holding of state receptions. Kemal Atatürk, founder and first president of Turkey, used Dolmabahçe as a presidential residence and died here on 10 November 1938. Facing the sea, the palace has a central building flanked by two wings, housing the State Room and the royal household. The building has more than 285 rooms, 43 large salons and six balconies. The palace houses the biggest crystal chandelier in the world, which hangs from the roof in the **State Room** and weighs 4½ tons. The centrepiece of the palace is the ornate, curved staircase leading to the **Salon of the Ambassadors**, the imperial reception

Dolmabahçe Palace gardens

room, with crystal and marble balusters. All clocks in the palace are set at 9:05, the moment that Atatürk died. During your visit, ask your guide to show you **Atatürk's Room**. His deathbed is draped with a Turkish flag. The secretariat and the parliamentary assembly of the Black Sea Economic Cooperation (BSEC), an 11-nation trade pact formed in 1992 and resembling the European Union, are located in the Harekât Kiosk, one of several ornate buildings within the grounds of Dolmabahçe Palace. Turkey, Greece, Bulgaria, Albania, Romania and six former Soviet republics are members of the BSEC.

From Dolmabahçe Palace, take a taxi uphill to **Taksim Square**, passing **İnönü Stadium**, **Istanbul Technical University**. Taksim is the hub of modern Istanbul and one of the principal bus terminals of the city. Taksim means 'distribution' in Turkish and gets its name from the squat structure on the west side of the square, the **Waterworks Department** (Sular Idaresi), where water was collected and distributed to this part of the city for centuries. The building no longer functions, but plans exist to turn it into a museum.

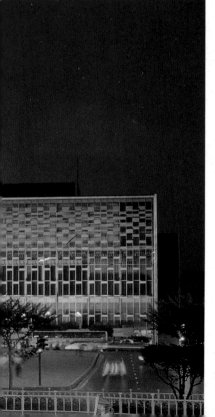

The tall building on the southern side of the square is the **Etap Marmara Hotel**, one of the city's five-star hotels. The modernistic building on the eastern side of the square is the **Atatürk Cultural Centre**, where opera performances and cultural events are produced during the annual summer Istanbul Festival. Taksim Park stands across from the Etap Marmara with the Sheraton rising in the background. The statue in the square, **Taksim Anıtı**, commemorates the founding of the Turkish Republic. It was erected in 1928. Numerous airline offices line **Cumhuriyet Caddesi** (Republic Avenue), the street that runs north of Taksim Park to the modern shopping neighbourhoods of **Nişantaşı**, **Osmanbey** and **Şişli**. The street that runs southwest from the square is

Taksim at night

Fashion shops in New Istanbul

Istiklâl Caddesi (Avenue of Independence), which has been turned into a pleasant walkway, along which trams operate. No cars are allowed on this avenue save for those belonging to the various foreign consulates. The avenue, known in the 19th century as the **Grand Rue de Pera**, runs through the shopping district known as Beyoğlu. A 10-minute ride on the noisy tram is a thrilling experience, especially for children, but to examine the buildings in more detail you will need to walk. The first building you come to on your right is the **French Consulate**, an 18th-century building that once served as a hospital to treat victims of the plague.

Take the first left, **Meşelik Caddesi**, which will bring you to **Aya Triadi**, the **Orthodox Church of the Holy Trinity**, the largest operating Greek church in Istanbul. The next interesting building you come to on your right is **Ağa Camii**, the only mosque in the entire Beyoglu district. The **Sakızağcı Caddesi**, the street that runs down the southern wall, takes you to the **Armenian Catholic Patriarchate**.

Number 158 on Istiklâl Caddesi is the **Cité d'Alep** with the magnificent **Ses Theatre**, founded in 1899 as a French variety show theatre. Restored in 1989 by Turkish comedian Ferhan Sensoy and his troupe, Ses Theatre is now the setting for musicals and cabaret performances.

Istiklâl Caddesi continues to **Galatasaray Square**, which gets its name from **Galatasaray Lisesi**, the second-oldest institution of learning in Istanbul after Istanbul University, which stands at the eastern side of the street. Described by Turks as **Mektebi Sultaniye**, the **Sultan's School**, the school was established in the late 15th century by Sultan Beyazìt II to train imperial pages, subordinate to the Palace School at Topkapı Sarayı. Galatasaray has played an enormous role in Turkey's modernisation and westernisation this century, producing a great number of graduates who became distinguished civil servants, politicians and diplomats.

Çiçek Pasajı, the Flower Passage

The ornate building diagonally across form the high school on the western side of Istiklâl Caddesi is **Çiçek Pasajı**, the **Flower Passage**, one of the most popular drinking spots in Istanbul. It is housed in the **Cité de Pera**, a baroque structure lined with colourful outdoor bistros, tavernas, and restaurants, where you can have lunch. The Cité was built in 1876. Notice the caryatids (support columns modelled on the female form) above the entrance. Sit outside to appreciate the sights, sounds and smells of the Pasaj. Stolling fiddlers and other musicians will perform at your table for a *bahşiş*, a tip. It is not uncommon to see half-dressed young men belly dancing with castanets to entertain visitors. Try to get Madam Anahit, a rotund, middle-aged Armenian woman, to perform French tunes on her accordion. Try some *meze* (appetisers), including shrimp and *kokoreç* (tasty, grilled lambs' intestines), washed down with beer and *rakı*. The end of the Pasaj opens to the **Galatasaray Fish and Flower Market** and leads to **Üç Horan Kilisesi**, one of Istanbul's two largest Ar-

menian churches, and a side street, **Sahne Sokak**, goes to the **British Consulate** (formerly the British Embassy), built in 1845 by Sir Charles Barry, the architect of the British Houses of Parliament.

Return to Galatasaray Square and walk across Istiklâl Caddesi. Turn back toward Taksim and take the first or second street to the right, walking to the **Galatasaray Hamamı**, one of Istanbul's leading Turkish baths. You should definitely take a bath at the *hamam*, as it is one of the luxuries of living or visiting Istanbul. Turkish baths primarily serve the common people whose homes have no baths or running water. Although the 15th-century Galatasaray Hamamı has separate men's and women's sections, foreign tour groups often rent it out for the entire afternoon or evening so that their members can mix. The management can arrange food and entertainment, such as women belly dancers, to be brought in from nearby restaurants and nightclubs for large groups. All big Turkish baths have three separate sections offering different temperatures: a *camekân*, or reception chamber with dressing rooms around a court where one recovers after a hot, steaming bath; the *soğukluk* or tepidarium, a room of intermediate temperature; and the *hararet*, or hot room, where one bathes. In its *hararet*, Galatasaray Hamamı has a *göbek* taşi, or round belly stone, where patrons lie down to be massaged and washed by *tellaks*, Turkish masseurs who wear rough rubbery gloves. After a good scrubbing from a *tellak*, you'll feel you've never been as clean in your life.

Afterwards return to Istiklâl Caddesi and walk south. About 50 metres/yards past Galatasaray Square, you will pass on your right the **Hacopulo Pasajı**, a 19th-century byway with a pleasant courtyard, leading from Istiklâl Caddesi to the British Consulate. A block away **Olivio Çıkmazı**, a cul-de-sac, leads to one of Istanbul's best restaurants, **Rejans**, founded after

In a Turkish bath

Services at the Church of St Anthony of Padua

World War 1 by a group of White Russian refugees. Rejans serves delicious *borsch*, *piroshky*, Chicken Kievsky, Peking Duck, *schnitzel*, with lemon vodka.

Return to Istiklâl Caddesi. Cross the street and come to the Franciscan **Church of St Anthony of Padua** (Sen Antuan in Turkish), the largest Catholic shrine in Istanbul. Less than 20,000 Catholics live in Turkey, almost all of them in Istanbul. A tiny chapel in the crypt of the church, reached by staircases to the left, on Sundays serves the tiny community of Chaldean Christians, who are members of the ancient Nestorian Church which is now in union with Rome. Chaldean-rite Catholics in Turkey are of Anatolian peasant stock. An estimated 5,000 Chaldean Christians live in Turkey, mainly in the mountains of southeast Turkey. Some 200 Chaldeans live in Istanbul today. In addition to Turkish, most Chaldeans speak Arabic. Their services are held in either Arabic or Aramaic, the ancient language of Jesus. The Catholic churches of Istanbul also allow the Syrian Orthodox (who have no chapels in Istanbul) to hold services in their churches at special hours.

Inside the church, on a wall by the altar, is a plaque commemorating Monsignor Angelo Giuseppe Roncalli, who lived in Istanbul and served as the apostolic delegate (diplomatic representative of the Pope) in Turkey from 1935 to 1944. Roncalli was elected pope in 1958, and took the name John XXIII.

Continuing along the eastern side of Istiklâl Caddesi, you come to the **Dutch Consulate**, built in 1855. The **Dutch Chapel**, one of two operating Protestant churches in Istanbul, is in a side street a short distance down the hill from the consulate.

Almost opposite the Dutch Consulate is **Odakule**, one of the tallest buildings of Istanbul with many business offices. Next door to Odakule is the popular **Garibaldi Bar Rotisserie** (Istiklâl Cad

The back streets of Istanbul

Odakule Yanı, Perukar Çıkmazı 1, Beyoğlu), located in a building near the site where Giuseppe Garibaldi (1807–82), the Italian patriot and revolutionary, lived in the 1830s while working as a captain of cargo ships sailing from the Mediterranean to the Black Sea. The building is owned by the Italian community, whose social club, **Societa Operaia Italiana**, on the top floor, is entered from the other end. The club is open on Thursday.

Turn back to Istiklâl Caddesi and cross the street once more and pass the Franciscan **Church of St Mary Draperis**, built in 1789. The church is reached by walking down a series of steps. A couple of blocks away is the **Russian Consulate**. If you take the first left down the hill, you will come to the **Crimean Memorial Church**, the largest Protestant church in Istanbul. It was constructed in

Gypsy players

1868 by Lord Stratford de Redcliffe and was designed by C. E. Street, the architect of the London Law Courts. The church was reopened in 1993.

Returning to Istiklâl Caddesi and walking down the street, you come to the **Swedish Consulate**, located in a pleasant park. Immediately opposite is **Narmanlı Han**, which once served as the old **Russian Embassy**, but now has several shops selling second-hand books and the offices of the Armenian-language daily newspaper *Jamanak*. Several bookshops, including **ABC**, **Haşet** and **Metro**, which sell foreign-language books can be found in this part of Istiklâl Caddesi.

You have now reached Istiklâl Caddesi's end, which is also the terminal point of the tram line and the Tünel. Stroll part way down **Galip Dede Caddesi**, which has shops selling stamps, musical instruments and old books, of which the best is the **Librairie de Pera** (Galip Dede Caddesi No 22, Tünel, tel: 2454998/2523078). The street gets its name from the **Mausoleum** (Türbe) **of Galip Dede**, a Mevlevi Dervish (member of a mystic Islamic religious order), on the left-hand side of the street. A *tekke*, or convent, of the Mevlevi brotherhood is located behind the mausoleum. The Whirling Dervishes of Konya often give performances in the convent.

Whirling Dervish

Behind the mausoleum, you can see the **Tomb of Kumbaracı** (Bombardier) **Ahmet Paşa**, the French officer Count Bonneval who joined the Ottoman Army during the reign of Mahmut I (1730–54) and was named Commandant of the Artillery Corps. Bonneval converted to Islam and adopted a Turkish name. He died in 1747. The cemetery of Ibrahim Müteferrika (1670–1745), the Turk who established the first Turkish printing press in the Ottoman Empire, is located close by.

Return to the end of Istiklâl Caddesi and follow the **Ilk Belediye Sokak**, the curving street that leads down from the Tünel past the **Beyoglu Municipality Building** to the **Turkish Airlines Terminal** in the district of **Sishane**. Take the first street on the left after passing the terminal. This is **Büyük Hendek Sokak** and you can see the **Galata Tower** straight ahead. You will walk by the **Neve Shalom Synagogue**, the biggest Jewish temple in Istanbul. On 6 September 1986, two gunmen belonging to the Abu Nidal group, an extremist Palestinian terrorist faction, attacked the synagogue during Friday prayers, killing 22 people, in the only day of tragedy in the 500-year history of the Jewish community in the city.

Have dinner at Galata Tower, a Genoese watchtower built in 1352 on the site of a wooden defence tower erected in 507 by the Byzantine Emperor Anastasius I (reigned 491–518). The 12-storey

tower is 61 metres (200ft) high. In the early 17th century, a Turkish daredevil, Hezarfen Ahmet Çelebi, took off from the top of the tower in an early hang-glider and flew across the Bosphorus. At first, Sultan Murat IV (1623–40) rewarded Çelebi, the first man to fly since the mythical Icarus, but then became suspicious and had him exiled to Algeria. There is a copper illustration of Çelebi's flight on the wall to the right of the ground-floor elevator.

From the round balcony of the tower, you get a stunning view of Istanbul. You can see the Golden Horn, the Galata

Galata Tower

and Atatürk bridges, Topkapı Palace, Haghia Sophia, the Blue Mosque, the Bosphorus and the Sea of Marmara. The **Galata Tower Restaurant** specialises in meat dishes, seafood and *mezes*, and has an exciting floor show with pop singers, folk music and belly dancing.

Belly dancer
Right, A typical fish restaurant
along the upper Bosphorus

Morning Itineraries

1. Around the Covered Bazaar

Begin at Çemberlitaş by visiting the Köprülü Mehmet Paşa Complex; walk by the Column of Constantine, Vezir Hanı and Nuruosmaniye Mosque; explore the Covered Bazaar.

Start your morning at **Çemberlitaş**, a noisy, crowded business district which is 600 metres (660 yards) west of Sultanahmet Park, for a tour of the Covered Bazaar and its environs. Çemberlitaş has numerous workshops (producing mainly leatherware, cotton-based fabrics and clothing), *lokantas* (poor men's restaurants) and cinemas that show Turkish films or foreign movies dubbed in Turkish. **Yeniçeriler Caddesi**, a continuation of Divanyolu, runs on an east-west axis through the district from Sultanahmet. Çemberlitaş means 'hooped column' in Turkish and it gets its name from the darkened **Column of Constantine**, which stands on the north side of the avenue. The column, which originally stood at the centre of the Forum built by Constantine the Great, was brought to the city in the fourth century from Rome. A statue of Constantine once stood on top of it.

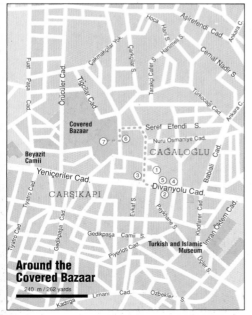

The building you see diagonally across the street is the 17th-century **Köprülü Mehmet Paşa Complex** with a mosque and *medrese* (theological school), established by Köprülü Mehmet Paşa, a member of an illustrious family of grand viziers. Five members of the Köprülü dynasty served as grand viziers in the 17th and 18th cen-

Legend:
1 *Column of Constantine*
2 *Köprülü Mehmet Paşa Complex*
3 *Atik Ali Paşa Camii*
4 *Vezir Hanı*
5 *Çemberlitaş Hamamı*
6 *Nuruosmaniye Camii*

Kapalı Çarsı, the Covered Bazaar

turies. Köprülü Mehmet Paşa is buried in a cemetery in the courtyard, as is Fuat Köprülü (1890–1966), a recent family member and Ottoman historian who served as foreign minister in the 1950s.

Atik Ali Paşa Camii, a 15th-century mosque, stands further west down Yeniçeriler Caddesi. **Çemberlitaş Hamamı**, a 16th-century Turkish bath that still operates, is just behind the column in Yeniçeriler Caddesi. From the column turn north and walk along Vezirhanı Caddesi toward **Nuruosmaniye Camii**, a 17th-century rococo mosque about 100 metres (330 ft) ahead. A short way down this street on your right, is **Vezir Hanı**, part of the Köprülü Complex. The 17th-century *han*, now in a severe state of dilapidation, once served as lodging for visiting merchants. Admire the Nuruosmaniye's unusual horseshoe-shaped courtyard, ornate exterior and curved sultan's ramp, even if you do not have time to visit. Nuruosmaniye has a fine *medrese*, which is now a students' dormitory, and there is also a library in its precincts.

One of the main entrances to the **Covered Bazaar**, or **Kapalı Çarşı** (Monday–Saturday 9am–7pm), the world's biggest emporium, is at the southwestern end of the Nuruosmaniye Mosque arcade. An oriental labyrinth of passageways and corridors, the Covered Bazaar has nearly 4,000 shops, 2,000 workshops and numerous *hans* making and selling everything: jewellery, carpets, antiques, ceramics, leatherware, shoes, furniture, alabaster, copper goods, tin products, silk fabrics, curtains, Lacoste T-shirts, Levi blue jeans and thousands of other items. The bazaar also has a dozen restaurants, 60 sandwich stands, two mosques, six

Carpet auction in the Old Bazaar

Souvenir hunting

mescits (small mosques), several barber shops and an Oriental coffeehouse.

An estimated 500,000 people shop there every day, both locals and foreign tourists. To avoid getting lost in its maze-like streets, always return to its main street, **Kalpakçılar Başı Caddesi**, the **Avenue of the Head Calpacmaker**, which runs through the Covered Bazaar in an east-west direction. Most trades are grouped together, as they were 530 years ago, when it was first constructed by Mehmet II after the Turkish conquest of Istanbul.

As you walk in an east-west direction along Kalpakçılar Başı Caddesi, you will notice **Sandal Bedesteni**, an enclosed area off the street, which was added in the 16th century and recently restored. The best time to visit the Sandal Bedesteni is on Monday and Thursday at 1am when hand-made carpets are auctioned.

Turn right at the second street that intersects Kalpakçılar Başı Caddesi, **Kuyumcular Caddesi**, and walk down. You will soon come to an interesting two-storey structure in the middle of the street. This former one-cubicle mosque is now a jewellery shop. If you turn right on Ağa Sokak, before reaching the cubicle mosque, and walk out of the bazaar, you come to the **Foreign Currency Black Market** on the corner of Cuhacı Hanı Sokağı, often described as the **Underground Central Bank**, because the millions of dollars that exchange hands daily here are unregistered with the authorities and go untaxed. You will notice hundreds of shops with no displays, but plain counters. The owners of these establishments are black marketeers. Their business of buying and selling foreign currency is conducted on the street among crowds of shouting men.

Return to the Covered Bazaar along Ağa Sokak and enter the **Old Bazaar**, **Eski Bedesteni**, one of the most dazzling sections of the emporium with its jewellers, antique dealers and carpet sellers. Afterwards return to the main street and leave the bazaar.

Getting a good buy

Window shopping

2. Around Saray Burnu

Visit the Museum of the Ancient Orient, the Archaeology Museum and the Tiled Kiosk Museum; take a stroll through Gülhane Parkı; walk up the Golden Horn. Explore Yeni Cami, the Spice Market and have lunch at Pandeli Restaurant.

Your morning begins at 9.30am with visits to the **Museum of the Ancient Orient** (open Sunday, Wednesday and Friday 9.30am–5pm) and the **Archaeology Museum** (Tuesday to Sunday 9.30am–5pm, closed Monday). The two are situated together, around a courtyard, between the First Court of Topkapı Palace and Gülhane Parkı. A third building, the **Tiled Kiosk Museum**

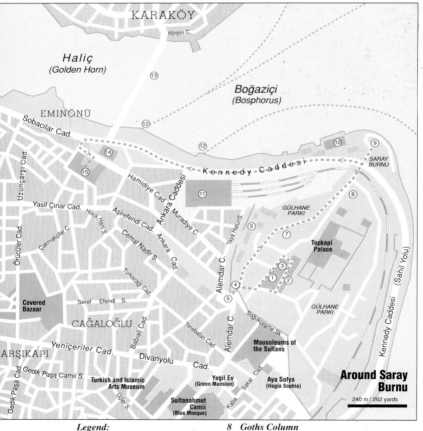

Legend:

1 Museum of the Ancient Orient	*8 Goths Column*
2 Archaeology Museum	*9 Atatürk Heykel*
3 Tiled Kiosk Museum	*10 International Press Centre*
4 Alay Köşkü	*11 Sirkeci Railway Station*
5 Sublime Porte	*12 Ferry Boat Landings*
6 Zoo	*13 Galata Bridge*
7 Tanzimat Museum	*14 New Mosque (Yeni Camii)*
	15 Egyptian Bazaar (Mısır Çarşısı)

(Sunday, Tuesday and Friday 9.30am–5pm), contains collections of 16th-century ceramics.

The Museum of the Ancient Orient, the first building in the courtyard, contains a unique collection of Babylonian, Sumerian, Hittite and Egyptian artifacts. It has a collection of more than 70,000 Sumerian and Arcadian cuneiform tablets, of which the **Treaty of Kadesh** is the most famous. Signed in 1269 BC between the Egyptian pharaoh and the Hittite King Hattusilis III, it is the earliest known peace treaty in the world. The collection of 13th-century BC sarcophagi with pharaohs' heads is impressive. One of these coffins holds the mummies of Bak-N-Mutand and his sacred cat. A pleasant outdoor coffeehouse, lined with old Greek columns and sarcophagi and sycamore trees, stands between the Museum of Ancient Orient and the Tiled Kiosk Museum.

Relaxing among the statues

Most of the 20 chambers of the **Archaeology Museum** are currently open to visitors. The museum is one of the best of its kind in the world, containing relics discovered in the Near East, dating from the prehistorical period to the end of the Byzantine era. The museum was founded in 1881 by Osman Hamdi Bey, one of Turkey's first archaeologists, best known for his excavations of the royal necropolis at Sidon, in present-day Lebanon. The centrepiece of the museum is the splendid **Alexander Sarcophagus**, discovered by Osman Hamdi Bey at Sidon. The sarcophagus did not belong to Alexander the Great but to an admirer of the Macedonian conqueror, possibly one of his generals. It gets

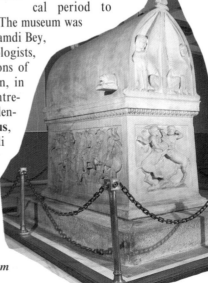

Lycean sarcophagus,
Archaeology Museum

View from Saray Burnu

its name from the friezes of Alexander the Great fighting with the Greek army against the Persians and hunting lions. Nearby is the equally impressive **Sarcophagus of Mourners**, shaped like a Greek temple with friezes of crying women on its sides and a hunting scene on top.

After a quick tour of the museums walk downhill to **GülhaneParkı**, once a part of the gardens of Topkapı Palace and now a grand public park. Step out of the massive gates on your left for a minute. The building you see across the street (**Alemdar Caddesi**) is the **State Security Court**, where political cases are tried. The building served, until a few years ago, as the city morgue. The ornate gate you see to the right is the back entrance to the **Provincial Capitol**, or **Vilayet Binası**, formerly the **Sublime Porte**, or **Bab-ı-ali**, which opened to the **Offices of the Grand Vizier** during Ottoman times. Return to Gülhane Parkì. The building you see to your left, on the top of the palace wall overlooking the street below is the **Alay Köşkü**, one of the pavilions of Topkapı Palace. It was used by sultans to review state processions. During his rule in the early 17th century, Ibrahim the Mad used the kiosk as a vantage point from which to shoot with his crossbow the pedestrians entering the Sublime Porte across the street.

As you walk through Gülhane Parkı you will see Istanbul's only zoo on your left. Its meagre menagerie includes mainly chickens, stray dogs and cats behind bars, but it also has vultures, eagles, goats, brown bears, peacocks, deer and camels. To your right, near the entrance to the park, are the busts of some of the former mayors of Istanbul. The tiny **Tanzimat Museum** (9.30am–4.30pm), which is further on to your right, displays the **Noble Rescript of the Rose Chamber**, or **Hatt-ı Şerif** of Gülhane, the most important document of Tanzimat reforms of the 19th century. The decree,

Fishing in Istanbul harbour

proclaimed by the sultan in 1839 at Gülhane Parkı, was a Bill of Rights granting all Ottoman citizens security of life, honour, property rights and equality of all religions in the application of Ottoman laws. The building that towers over the inner wall of Topkapı Palace to your right is a part of the Harem. It is the Kiosk of Osman III, sultan 1754–7. Near the end of the park, a trail leads right to the so-called **Goths Column**, set up sometime between AD 268 and 270 to celebrate Claudius II Gothicus's victory over the Goths. According to one Byzantine historian, a statue of Byzas, the mythical founder of the city, stood on the top of it.

Slicing fish

When you reach the end of the park, cross the railway and the street, Kennedy Caddesi, named after John F Kennedy. You have now reached **Saray Burnu**, or **Palace Point**, a park at the confluence of the Golden Horn, the Bosphorus and the Sea of Marmara. A statue of Atatürk (1881–1938), creator and first president of the Turkish Republic, stands in the park. The monument, which was completed in 1926 by Austrian sculptor Heinrich Krippel, was the first statue of a human being ever erected in Turkey, a representation that angered Islamic fundamentalists. From Saray Burnu, turn left, keep to the pavement, and follow the Golden Horn, or Haliç, an 8-km-long and 400-metre-wide (5 miles by 400 yards) inlet to the Bosphorus, where the city's har-bour is located. Once lined with palace

View from the Galata Bridge

gardens, public parks, churches and mosques, and described by poets as **Sadabad**, or place of bliss, the Golden Horn has become an open cesspool. More than a quarter of the city's sewage and industrial waste spew into its waters, turning the water an ugly grey and creating a stench that many of the 1.6 million people who live close by claim burns their eyes and throats.

In the mid-1980s, initiatives were taken to clean up the Golden Horn. The municipality has demolished 1,200 buildings, including 400 factories, that dumped pollutants into the Golden Horn, and built new parks and playgrounds along its shores. A new underground sewage collection system prevents waste from polluting its waters. Thanks to this programme of urban renewal, you can now walk from Saray Burnu to the end of the Golden Horn, without having to take any detours.

The first building you come to on your right is **Sepetçiler Kasrı**, or **Palace of the Basket Weavers**, a 17th-century building that was part of Topkapı Palace grounds. The building now serves as the International Press Centre. The building gets its original name from the fact that the mad Sultan, Deli Ibrahim, spent long days here weaving baskets – his favourite hobby. Across the street is the **Sirkeci Railway Station**, the terminus of the Orient Express. The

Selling old titles

Afternoon Itineraries

3. Student Days

Begin at Sahaflar Çarşısı, the second-hand booksellers' market just off the Covered Bazaar; pass Beyazıt Camii, the Public Library and Beyazıt Square; stroll through the main campus of Istanbul.

This afternoon programme takes you on a tour of Istanbul University and its surroundings. Start at the **Old Book Bazaar** or **Sahaflar Çarşısı** just off the main western exit of the Covered Bazaar.

You can buy many second-hand books in this bazaar, lined with bookshops. The **Bust of Ibrahim Müteferika**, who printed the first works in Turkish in 1732, stands in the centre of the courtyard. The book bazaar opens onto the **Beyazıt Square**, one of the biggest in Istanbul. The square gets its name from the imposing 16th-century **Beyazıt Camii** to your left. In its precincts, you can see the *türbes* (mausoleums) of Sultan Beyazıt II (sultan 1481–1512), his daughter Selçuk Sultan, and of Grand Vizier Koca Reşit Paşa, the leader of the Tanzimat reform movement, who died in 1857. To your right is the **State Library** (Devlet Kütüphanesi), once a public kitchen that served food to the poor.

Once in the square proper, the arch you see to your right is the entrance to the main campus of **Istanbul University**, one of the great institutions of learning in the world. The campus stands on the grounds of the first palace of Mehmet II, which later served as the Ministry of War. The **Beyazıt Tower**, used as a fire watchtower

Old Book Bazaar

Legend:
1 Old Book Bazaar
2 Beyazıt Camii
3 State Library
4 Beyazıt Square
5 Istanbul University
6 Beyazıt Tower
7 Süleymaniye (Mosque Complex
  of Süleyman the Magnificent)
8 Tomb of Süleyman
  the Magnificent
9 Tomb of Hürrem Sultan
10 Tomb of Sinan

Student Days

160 m / 175 yards

Haliç
(Golden Horn)

Ragip Gümüşpala Caddesi

Hacı Kadın Cad.

KÜÇÜKPAZAR

Kible Çeşme C.

Kutucular Cad.

Ord. Prof. Cemil Bilsel C.

Vefa Cad.

Fetva Yok

Mimar Sinan Cad.

VEFA

Uzunçarşı Cad.

Kirazlı Mescit S.

Süleymaniye C.

Beşim Ömer Paşa

Prof. Sıddık Sami Onar Cad.

İsmetiye Cad.

Nargelekci S.

Fuat Paşa Cad.

Oruçular Cad.

Bozdoğan Kemeri Cad.

Cad.

BEYAZIT

Ahmet Paşa S.

Vezneciler C.

Üniversite Cad.

Bakırcılar C.

Ordu Caddesi

Yeniçeriler Cad.

Turanlı S.

Tiyatro Cad.

ÇARŞIKAPI

and as a meteorology station, is by the main building.

Walk along the outer western walls of the university to the **Süleymaniye**, the Mosque Complex of Süleyman the Magnificent. The second largest mosque in Istanbul but by far the most magnificent and graceful, the Süleymaniye is a testimony to the greatest ruler of the Ottoman Empire. Under Süleyman, the Ottoman Empire reached its apex of power. The mosque dominates the third hill of old Istanbul, surrounded by the *külliye*, comprising *medreses*, a *caravansary*, a *hamam* and a shopping arcade. The mosque, completed in 1557, was the work of Mimar Sinan, the greatest Ottoman architect. The *külliye* was finished later by Sinan.

The mosque stands in the centre of a vast outer courtyard ringed on three sides by a wall with grilled windows. A porticoed *avlu* (courtyard) precedes the mosque. The shrine has four minarets traditionally said to represent the fact that Süleyman was the fourth sultan to reside in Istanbul. The 10 balconies, or *serifes*, of the minarets indicate that he was the 10th sultan to reign. The vast interior conveys both simplicity and grandeur. Its centralised dome stands 47 metres (156ft) above the ground. Behind the mosque is

the octagonal **Türbe of Süleyman the Magnificent** (sultan 1520–66). The smaller tombs are those of his beloved daughter, the Princess Mihrimah, and two later sultans, Süleyman II (1687–91) and Ahmet II (1691–5).

East of Süleyman's mausoleum is the **Türbe of Hürrem Sultan**, Süleyman's favourite wife who died in 1558, known in the west as Roxelana, 'the Russian'. Her influence over Süleyman was so great that she persuaded him to kill his own son, Mustafa, on the pretext that he was planning to usurp the throne. Mustafa's death allowed Roxelana's son, Selim the Sot, to succeed to the throne. Western histories date the start of the Ottoman Empire's decline to Selim's alcoholic rule.

4. A Religious Walkway

Tour the upper reaches of the Golden Horn. Start from Rüstem Paşa Camii and pass the Atatürk Bridge; visit the Orthodox Church Patriarchate. Taxi to Kariye Camii; walk along the Byzantine Land Walls to Tekfur Sarayı, the Palace of Blachernae, the Walls of Leo and Heraclius and the Holy Ayazma.

The Grand Vizier's Mosque: Begin on a side street off to the left of **Ragıp Gümüşpala Caddesi** 100 metres (110 yards) from the Spice Market to visit the **mosque of Rüstem Paşa**. The mosque was built by Mimar Sinan in 1561 for Rüstem Paşa, twice grand vizier under Süleyman the Magnificent and husband of the sultan's favourite daughter, Mihrimah Sultan. The mosque, built on a high terrace

Süleymaniye Mosque interior

over a complex of shops, is famous for its blue-tiled interior. Return to Ragıp Gümüşpala Caddesi and cross to the Golden Horn side of the street with its parks. You will see two old commercial buildings or *hans*, the bigger of which is **Zindan Han**, or **Prison Han**, once a women's prison and now a tourist shopping centre with a top-floor restaurant that has a panoramic view of Istanbul harbour. Nearby is the **Ahi Çelcbi Mosque**, built in the 15th century. The modernistic building you next pass is the **Istanbul Chamber of Commerce**. You soon come to the **Atatürk Bridge**, another pontoon spanning the Golden Horn. On the hill to your left is the **Aqueduct of Valens**, built in the fourth century by Roman Emperor Valens. Continue past the Atatürk Bridge. In this section of the city, parts of the Byzantine sea walls remain intact though houses and workshops have been built along their sides.

The white building you see on the left is the state-owned **Cibali Cigarette Factory**. If you look across the Golden Horn, you can see the **Cami-altı and Taskızak Shipyards**, which have existed here for more than 500 years. The palatial white building you see near the shore was once the Ministry of War. It now serves as the **Regional Naval**

Legend:
1 *Rüstem Paşa Camii*
2 *Istanbul Chamber of Commerce*
3 *Atatürk Bridge*
4 *Gül Camii (Mosque of Roses)*
5 *Orthodox Church Patriarchate*
6 *Greek High School*
7 *Church of St Mary of the Mongols*
8 *Bulgarian Church*
9 *Metochion of Mount Sinai*
10 *Ahrida Synagogue*
11 *Feruh Kathuda Mosque*
12 *Old Galata Bridge*
13 *Kariye Mosque*
14 *Tekfur Sarayı*
15 *Crooked Gate*
16 *Blachernae Palace*

A Religious Walkway
320 m / 350 yards

EYÜP

DEFTIERDAR
Boğaziçi Köprüsü Çevre Yolu

Rami - Kışla Cad.

AYVANSARAY

Ayvansaray Cad.

Savaklar Caddesi

Şişhane C. Cad.

Hocaçakir Cad.   Hocaçakir

Fevzi Paşa Cad.

Salma Tomruk Cad.

Kariye Camii

Demirhisar Cad.

Püsküllü C.

Vefa Stadyumu (Stadium)

Draman Cad.

Ayan S.

BALAT

Mürsel Paşa Cad.

FENER

Haliç (Golden Horn)

Fethiye C.

Yıldırım Cad.

Camcı Çeşmesi

Sultan Selim Camii

Yavuz Selim Cad.   Caddesi

Darüşşafaka Cad.

Haliç Caddesi   Aykapı Cad.

Kara Sarıklı Sokağı

Fevzi Paşa Cad.

Haliç Caddesi

Sair Nabi S.

Fatih Camii

Abdülezelpaşa Cad.

Civali Cad.

Büyük Karaman C.

Haydar Cad.

UNKAPANI

Macar Kardeşler Cad.

Aqueduct of Valens

Atatürk   Bulvarı   Atatürk Köprüsü

Itfaiye Cad.

Hacı Kadın Cad.

KÜÇÜKPAZAR

Atatürk Bulvarı

Şehzade Başı Cad.

VEFA

Şehzade Camii   Vefa Cad.

Ragıp Gümüşpala Cad.

Kıble C.C.

Belediye Sarayı (Palace)

Kıraz M.S.

Süleyman Camii

Fevzia Yok.

BEYAZIT

Süleymaniye C.

Minar S.C.

EMINÖNÜ

Istanbul University

Ömer Paşa Cad.

Ordu Cad.

Üniversite C.

Besim Ömer Paşa Cad.

University

Ismetiye Cad.

Uzunçarşı C.

Oruçcular Cad.

Vasıf Çınar C.

Hasırcılar C.

Yeni Camii (New Mosque)

Mısır Çarşısı

Street in Fener

Command, **Kuzey Saha Komutanlığı**. The building on the hill is the **Naval Hospital**.

You soon come to **Cibali Kapısı**, one of the principal sea gates of Byzantine walls. It gets its name from Cebe Ali Bey, the Turkish officer whose troops breached the wall at this point during the Ottoman conquest of Istanbul in 1453. A building to its right between two roads is known as **Constantine's Bath** and is said to have been constructed in the fourth century, but no one knows why it was built outside the walls.

About 270 metres (300 yards) past Cibali Kapısı is **Aya Nikola**, the 18th-century **church of St Nicholas**. This church was originally the *metochion*, or private property, of the Vatopedi Monastery on Mount Athos, in northeastern Greece. Beyond Aya Nikola is the **Aya Kapısı**, the **Holy Gate**. Enter the gate and take the second street on the left and you come to the imposing **Gül Camii**, or Mosque of Roses, formerly the Orthodox **Church of St Theodosia**. The 12th-century church was dedicated to Theodosia, a woman martyred during the Iconoclast period for her opposition to the destruction of church icons. When the Ottomans conquered the city, they discovered a large Greek congregation praying inside the church, which was decked with roses – hence the name. It was one of many churches in the city that the Turks turned into mosques.

Back on the main street, you reach the district of **Fener** (Phanar) and the **Orthodox Church Patriarchate**, which has been on this site since 1601. Considering that it is the symbolic spiritual centre of the world's 200 million Orthodox Christians the Patriarchate is a modest establishment. From Fener, the Patriarch wields influence over Orthodox churches in Crete, the Dodecanese Islands, the monastic community of Mount Athos in Greece, the United States, Canada, Australia, New Zealand, South America and Western Europe. The patriarchate includes the **Church of St George** and a number of old buildings and newly built offices.

Entrance to the Patriarchate is by **Sadrazam Ali Pasa Caddesi** just off Abdülezel Paşa Caddesi, the street that runs along the Golden Horn. On entering, you will notice that the main gate is permanently welded shut and painted black. This is the famous **Orta Kapı**, the Central Door, and it has been the sign of Greek-Turkish intransigence for centuries. It was on this spot that Patriarch Gregory V was hanged for treason in 1821, the beginning of the Greek War of Independence from the Ottoman Empire.

The Church of St George dates from 1720. Above its main entrance is a two-headed eagle with its wings spread out, one holding the cross and the other holding a crown, representing the spiritual and temporal powers of the Patriarch and the Byzantine emperors. Inside the cavern-like church you can see many icons, darkened from the soot of candles. The most impressive item inside is a golden mosaic of the Virgin Mary and Christ. The sarcophagi of several early saints are located along the southern wall.

Once a flourishing Greek neighbourhood, Fener has decayed into a slum, but it does contain many Greek churches and schools of interest. Now only a few elderly Greek couples who work at the Patriarchate live in this old neighbourhood – a sad reminder of its once illustrious past. Beginning in the 16th century Greek families of the neighbourhood, the Phenariots, amassed huge fortunes from trade and commerce and wielded considerable influence on the Ottoman Empire's foreign affairs. These Phenariots, drawn primarily from 11 wealthy Greek families, acquired high positions, such as principal interpreters of the sultan and the *Kaputan Derya*, the grand admiral of the Ottoman fleet. They became *de facto* governors of the Aegean Islands, from whose Greek citizens the crews of the Ottoman navy came. The most influential position held by the Phenariots was the *Hospodar*, or prince, of the Danubian principalities of Moldavia and Walachia. The wealth they acquired from these two provinces was channelled back to Fener, where they built grand palaces and luxurious homes, traces of which can still be seen. In recent years, Anatolian peasants have replaced the Greeks.

On the same street as the Patriarchate, 45 metres (50 yards) to the northeast, you can see the palatial **Özel Maraşlı Rum Ilkokulu**, a Greek primary school whose seven students are bussed from other

structed in 1835, and **Feruh Kuthuda Camii**, a mosque built by Mimar Sinan in the 16th century.

Balat is a Turkish corruption of the word *palation*, or palace, and is derived from the presence of Blachernae Palace, the last residence of the Byzantine emperors, traces of which can be seen along the Byzantine land walls. You will walk along these walls later.

Now, return to the shore to visit the Old Galata Bridge. The green-coloured pontoon crossing was built in 1912 at the site of the new Galata Bridge. It was dismantled after a fire destroyed a section and relocated to the present site.

Hail a taxi in Balat to your next destination, **Kariye Camii**, the **Church of St Saviour in Chora**, located near **Edirne Kapı**, one of the main gates along the Byzantine land walls.

Mosaic, Kariye Camii

Kariye Camii is the most fascinating church in Istanbul after Hagia Sophia because of its brilliant mosaics and frescoes, many of which are the finest masterpieces of Christian religious art in the world. The mosaics and paintings portray the lives of the Virgin Mary and Christ.

The church itself is not of much architectural interest. The Greek name of the church, *Chora*, means 'in the country'. It gets this name from the fact that it was originally located in the countryside, outside the city walls built by Constantine the Great. But after the walls were extended by Constantine's successors, the church stood within the city walls. The present church, built by the mother-in-law of the Byzantine Emperor Alexius I Comnenus, dates from the late 11th century. The frescoes and paintings were made from 1315–21 by the artist Grand Logethete Theodore Metochites, whose mosaic stands in the mural above the door to the nave. It shows him offering the church to the enthroned Christ. In the early 16th century, the Turks converted the church into a mosque, covering the paintings and mosaics with plaster. But the artwork has been restored and now Kariye Camii is a museum. The houses and streets in the museum's immediate surroundings have been restored by Çelik Gülersoy and his Automobile and Touring Association. Gülersoy has built the pleasant **Kariye Hotel** and the **Kariye Cafes**, which includes the authentic, old Turkish **Muhallebici Salonu**, or **Pudding Shop**.

There are more than 100 mosaics and frescoes in Kariye Camii. The mosaics are arranged in the following six groups and should be viewed in that order:

– the six large dedicatory or devotional panels in the outer narthex and inner narthex, which include the **Portraits of St Paul and St**

Peter (to the left and right of the nave) and the so-called **Deesis**, which shows Christ with his mother;
– the genealogy of Christ in the northern and southern domes of the inner narthex, one of which portrays a medallion of **Christ Pantocrator and His Ancestors**;
– the cycle of the Blessed Virgin in the first three bays of the inner narthex;
– the cycle of the infancy of Christ, which includes the stunning **Three Wise Men**. Each of the 13 mosaics occupies a mural in the outer narthex;
– the cycle of Christ's ministry occupying the domed vaults of all seven bays of the outer narthex as well as parts of the south bay of the inner narthex;
– the panels in the Nave, which include the realistic **Dormition of the Virgin**, portraying the Virgin Mary dead. Christ stands behind holding her soul, represented as a babe in swaddling clothes. The apostles, evangelists and early bishops of the church surround them. Hovering over the scene are six angels.

The frescoes are in the **Parecclesion**, a kind of enclosed aisle to the right of the church. These show:
– scenes from the resurrection, including the **Anastasis**, one of the greatest paintings in the world. The Anastasis shows Christ breaking the gates of Hell, which lie beneath his feet, while Satan lies bound before him. With his right hand he pulls Adam out of his tomb. Behind Adam stand St John the Baptist, David, Solomon and other biblical kings. With his left he pulls Eve out of her tomb, in which stands Abel;
– the Last Judgment with scenes from heaven and hell;
– the 27 saints and the martyrs.

Old city walls

Tekfur Sarayı

A number of tombs exist in the walls of the Pareeclesion, including that of Theodore Metochites, traces of which can still be seen.

After you have viewed the mosaics and paintings, leave the church and walk up to the Byzantine city walls, just a block away, and follow them down the hill to the Golden Horn. You will see just a small part of the land walls, which are 7km (4¼ miles) in length, extending from the Sea of Marmara to the Golden Horn. Most of the walls are now in ruins. For more than 1,000 years, until breached by the Crusaders in 1204 and by the Ottoman Turks 250 years later, the walls kept successive invaders from capturing Constantinople. The land walls were 5 metres (16ft) thick and towered 12 metres (16½ ft) above the city. They were guarded by 96 towers. The Byzantines built magnificent houses and palaces along the walls. Today these have all but disappeared, replaced by shanties or *gecekondu* dwellings, hovels built overnight by Anatolian peasants who have migrated to Istanbul.

As you walk down the hill, the first sight is the **Tekfur Sarayı**, or **Palace of the Sovereign**, which was perhaps an appendage to Blachernae Palace. Only the facade of the building, erected in the late 13th century or early 14th century, remains. After the Turkish conquest it became a zoo, particularly for large animals such as elephants and giraffes, and later it was used as a brothel. In 1719, famous Tekfur pottery was produced in kilns built inside Tekfur Sarayı. In the early 19th century it served as a poorhouse for local Jews. Now it is a museum. **Eğrikapı**, the **Crooked Gate**, is one of

Byzantine walls

the many gates along the land walls. It gets its name because the narrow lane which enters the city must skirt around a mausoleum, which is almost in front of the gate. This funerary is believed to be the **Türbe of Hazreti Hafız**, a companion of Mohammed who was killed near this spot during the first Arab siege of Constantinople. The burial place was only discovered in the 18th century and the mausoleum was built blocking the road.

Another 200 metres (220 yards) downhill brings one to **Ivaz Efendi Camii**, a mosque built in the late 16th century. The mosque is the site on which the **Palace of Blachernae**, the last residence of the Byzantine emperors, once stood. Only traces of the palace remain. It was destroyed long ago by fires and the building of a shanty town over the site. The tower you see behind the mosque was where deposed emperors were imprisoned and tortured. The far end of the mosque court by the tower ends in a sudden, precipitous drop of nearly 100 metres, and should be avoided. A modern concrete stairway behind the mosque is said to lead to rooms and hallways inside the palace, but unless you have a guide and flashlight it might be too dangerous to enter.

The terrace-cum-public park in front of the mosque gives a spectacular view of the end of the Byzantine walls and the upper reaches of the Golden Horn. If you continue to walk down the hill, following the land walls, you soon come to the impressive red brick **Walls of Leo and Heraclius** with their massive towers. Between the walls is a citadel, in which you can see a small Muslim graveyard containing the **Tombs of Ebu Seybet ül-Hudri and Hemd ül-Ensari**, two other Arab warrior companions of the Prophet Mohammed who were killed

Golden Horn

during a seventh-century Arab siege of Constantinople.

Nearby is the ancient **Ayazma of Blachernae** (Holy Spring of St Basil), the holiest spot in Byzantine Constantinople. It is located in a modern Greek chapel, surrounded by a court in the Balat-Ayvansaray region. It is open on Sundays, but you might be able to persuade the janitor to open its doors on other days.

Hail a taxi and return to Eminönü and have dinner at Hamdi Et Lokantasi (Tahmis Cad, Kalçcin Sok 17). The restaurant, which specialises in spicy kebabs of southeast Turkey, is located behind the car park next to the spice market. Try its summer speciality – aubergine kebab served with *meze* appetizers.

5. The Holy District of Eyüp

Begin at the Eyüp Mosque; visit the Mausoleum of Eyüp Ensari, the Complex of Mihrişah Sultan, the Mausoleums of Mehmet V Reşat and Sokollu Mehmet Paşa; walk to the Complex of Zal Mahmut; taxi to Pierre Loti's Coffeehouse for afternoon tea; walk down to Eyüp along the Cemetery, visiting the Tomb of Field Marshal Fevzi Çakmak.

Spend a lazy afternoon exploring the sacred district of Eyüp, along the upper reaches of the Golden Horn.

Eyüp is a vast necropolis with *türbes* (mausoleums) of Ottoman sultans, prominent prime ministers, soldiers and religious men and their families, surrounding **Eyüp Sultan Mosque**, one of the holiest Islamic sites in the world. The mosque contains the **Mausoleum of Eyüp Ensari**, the companion and standard bearer of the Prophet Mohammed. Eyüp was killed during the first Arab siege of Constantinople between 674 and 678. His cemetery was discovered eight centuries later, after the Ottoman conquest, and his mausoleum was erected at this site.

It is to Eyüp Sultan Mosque that Istanbul families bring their young boys, decked in white uniforms and red caps, before ritual circumcision. Mehmet II, the sultan who conquered Istanbul, constructed the mosque complex, which includes the mausoleum, mosque, *medrese*, *han*, *hamam*, *imaret* and market, in 1458. By the 18th century, Mehmet II's original foundation for the mosque was in ruins and Sultan Selim III had a new building erected in 1798.

In the hills overlooking Eyüp are sprawling shanty towns and the large **Eyüp Cemetery** filled with old Ottoman tombs with headstones shaped like turbans. It's still considered a privilege to be buried here.

Behind Eyüp Sultan Mosque facing the Golden Horn is the **Complex of Mihrişah Sultan**, a

Young candidates for ritual circumcision

gigantic *külliye* constructed by Mirisah Valide Sultan in 1794 which includes the mausoleum of the founder, a *mektep* (primary school), an *imaret* (public kitchen), and splendid water fountains. Nearby is a series of *türbes*, including the **Mausoleum of Mehmet V Reşat**, sultan 1909–18, which is closed to the public. The tombs of several Ottoman prime ministers are located at the intersection, including the **Mausoleum of Sokollu Mehmet Paşa**. The son of a Bosnian priest, Sokollu entered the palace school as a young man and married Esmahan Sultan, daughter of Selim the Sot. An able statesman, he held many high positions, including the post of grand vizier in the closing years of Süleyman's reign. Unfortunately he was assassinated by a madman. He was one of the main characters portrayed in Nobel Prize winner Ivo Andric's novel *The Bridge Over the Drina*. The mausoleum, a work of Mimar Sinan, is now part of a medical dispensary.

From here walk to the **Mosque Complex of Zal Mahmut**, approximately 400 metres/yards to the northeast. Zal was an executioner. An influential man, he succeeded in having Prince Mustafa, the son of Süleyman the Magnificent, put to death on trumped-up charges of treason. He later became a prominent official of substantial wealth and married the Princess Şah Sultan, another daughter of Selim the Sot, as a reward for his services. The mosque and courtyard are built on split levels. The lower level includes the **Türbes of Zal Mahmut and Princess Şah Sultan** and a *medrese* (theological seminary). The mosque, together with another *medrese,* is located on the upper levels.

Turkish cemetery

Now take a taxi to **Pierre Loti's Coffeehouse** on the hill above Eyüp for afternoon tea. This coffeehouse was made famous by Pierre Loti (1850–1923), a French novelist and Turcophile who lived in Eyüp for several years. Watch the sun set over the Golden Horn, then walk through the cemetery to Eyüp, stopping to look at the cemetery stones with their turban tops. A short distance from the coffeehouse, just off the main trail to the right, visit the **Tomb of Field Marshal Fevzi Çakmak** (1876–1950), a heroic army commander during World War 1 and the Turkish War of Independence and chief-of-staff of the Turkish Armed Forces from 1921 to 1944.

Eating Out

It will take a lifetime to discover all the finest restaurants and eateries of Istanbul. Turkish cuisine ranks among the three best in the world – the other two being Cantonese and French. Turkish food reflects the tastes of the Ottoman Empire, which stretched from the gates of Vienna to the deserts of Arabia.

Grab a kebab

The Turkish palate favours the spicy kebabs of southern Anatolia, the tender lamb dishes of Central Asia, the steaks (*biftek* and *bonfile*) of Western Europe, and the *meze* appetisers of the Aegean and Mediterranean coasts. Residents of Istanbul delight in the tasty fish and seafood caught all along the Bosphorus, the Sea of Marmara and the Black Sea. Look out also for seasonal fresh fish. Some of the best fish caught in the area includes *kalkan* (turbot) and *lüfer* (blue fish), a meaty fish caught in winter. Fried *barbunya* (striped mullet) is also best in winter. Below is a list of suggested restaurants found on or around the routes in this book. Guidelines are given on prices: inexpensive signifies $16-20 for two, excluding wine; moderate, $21–40; and expensive $41 plus.

In Old Istanbul

FIRAT RESTAURANT
Çakaktaş Sok 11A
Kumkapı
Tel: (0212) 5172308
Inexpensive Turkish cuisine.

ALTIN KUPA RESTAURANT
Yebatan Cad 6, Sultanahmet
Tel: (0212) 519 4770
Specialises in fish. Inexpensive.

HAMDI ET LOKANTASI
Tahimis Cad
Kalça Sok No 17, Eminönü
Tel: (0212) 5280390/5125424
Good kebabs. Inexpensive.

HAVUZLU RESTAURANT
Gani Çelebi Sok PTT Yani 3
Kapalıçarşı
Tel: (0212) 5273346
This is the best of the restaurants to be found in the Covered Bazaar. It specialises in kebabs and delicious *meze* appetisers. Prices are inexpensive.

KÖR AGOP RESTAURANT
Ördekli Bakkal Sok No 7
Kumkapı
Tel: (0212) 5172334, 5172335
A justly famous Armenian-owned fish restaurant in a colourful setting. Expensive.

PANDELI RESTAURANT
Mısır Çarşısı
Eminönü
Tel: (0212)5225534
Serves excellent fish and meat dishes in an historic setting. Moderate prices.

KONYALI
Topkapı Palace
Tel: (0212) 5139696
Konyalı is known for its delicious lamb specialities and vegetable dishes. Moderate.

KONUK EVI
Soğukçeşme Sok
Sultanahmet
Tel: (0212) 5140216
Serves Turkish cuisine at moderate prices.

OLIMPIYAT 2 MINAS RESTAURANT
Samsa Sok 7
Kumkapi
Tel: (0212) 5172237
Long-established fish restaurant in colourful Armenian quarter of the city. Moderate.

SARNIÇ RESTAURANT
Soğukçeşme Sok
Sultanahmet
Tel: (0212) 2314631
Turkish cuisine. This restaurant occupies a cavernous Roman cistern – making it especially attractive to diners during the hot summer months.

ÜÇLER BALIK RESTAURANT
Ördekli Bakkal Sok 3
Kumkapı
Tel: (0212) 5172336
This is a famous Albanian-owned restaurant specialising in fish. In-expensive.

SULTAN PUB RESTAURANT
Divan Yolu 2
Sultanahmet
Tel: (0212) 5266347
Inexpensive. European food. Near Blue Mosque.

On the Bosphorus

CLUB 29
Paşabahçe Yolu
Cubuklu
Tel: (0212) 3223888
Expensive restaurant cum bar, plus swimming pool and disco. Stunning setting on the Asian side of the Bosphorus. Summer only.

CLUB 29
Nispetiye Cad 29
Etelier
Tel: (0212) 2635411
Fashionable bar and restaurant. Open winter only.

LIVAR RESTAURANT
Kuruçeşme Cad 104
Kuruçeşme
Tel: (0212) 2656294, 2657940
Good seafood.

Pastries anyone?

Istanbul at night

by phone to the three-inch rusted key, purportedly left by the author, claiming it would open a chest containing a diary of her 11-day disappearance. According to Rand, a producer at Warner Brothers Studios who was making a movie about Christie's disappearance had asked her to make the call and help trace the key. Matters became more complicated when Hasan Süzer, chairman of the hotel, snatched the key and offered to sell it for $2 million. After years of unsuccessful negotiations with Warner Brothers, the key is still with the Süzer family and Agatha Christie's last mystery remains unravelled.

Pera Palas's **Orient Bar**, with its comfortable sofas and chairs, has changed little since the Orient Express first pulled into Istanbul almost a century ago.

The next place on the agenda is **Taksim Sanat Evi** (Sıraselviler Cad 69/1, Taksim), off Taksim Square. This bar-restaurant, which has a stunning view of the Bosphorus and live music after 8pm, is a favourite gathering place for Turkish yuppies. You can have a drink and then walk over to **Bilsak** (Sıraselviler Cad, Soğanlı Sok 7, Cihangir), 120 metres/135 yards away on a side street opposite the Taksim Ilk Yardım Hastanesi (Taksim Emergency Hospital). Bilsak has two bars, which are gathering places of die-hard Communists, intellectuals, feminists, Greens, the gay community and other marginal groups in the city.

Walk back toward Taksim Square and turn left at the building that houses the provincial headquarters of Anavatan Partisi and Sosyal Demokrat Halkçı Parti, the two main political parties in Turkey. Take the first left from there and walk about 50 metres/55 yards) and you come to **Çiçek Bar** (Bilurcu Sok 25, Sıraselviler Cad), indisputably the best bar in Istanbul. Çiçek Bar is a colourful and friendly place where journalists, film-makers, actors, advertising

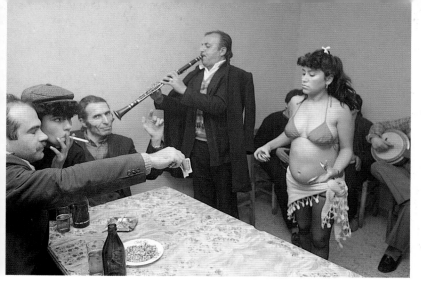

Belly dancing for a living

agency executives and intellectuals congregate to have drinks and
hammer out business deals. It can appear a bit clubby, but don't
be daunted – you can usually get in if you ask. Çiçek Bar, also
known as Arif'in Yeri or Arif's Place, was founded by the Association
of Cinema Lovers.

For those interested in the seedier aspects of the city, the back
streets of Beyoğlu (areas that are parallel to Istiklâl Caddesi) offer
thousands of sleazy bars, nightclubs and pubs with belly dancing,
sad *a la Turca* (Oriental) music and all forms of naughty nightlife.
The ultimate experience of sleaze in Istanbul is a visit to the *genel
evs*, or public brothels, at **Zürafa Sokak** (Giraffe Street), near
Karaköy just off Yüksek Kaldırım Sokak, the avenue that runs
down the hill from one end of Istiklâl Caddesi to the port district
of Karaköy. The brothels are, in fact, scores of illuminated apartment
buildings in an enclosed area.

To top off a night in Istanbul, take a taxi to Gayrettepe, in the
new city, to visit the bar-restaurant **Zeytin and Sardunya** (Yildiz
Posta Cad 25; tel: (0212) 2748713/2886439). Here you can listen
to a combination of French songs and Turkish pop, performed by
soloists Atilla Demircan and Nurcan Eren in a friendly atmosphere.
Don't arrive too early – Zeytin and Sardunya comes to life around
11pm and operates until the early morning hours. The bar serves
excellent margaritas.

Late night jazz

Shopping

Istanbul is a shopper's delight. The best of Turkey's hand-woven wool and silk Anatolian carpets, leatherware, ceramics, gold and silver jewellery, modern miniatures, alabaster figurines, meerschaum pipes, and antiques can be bought in the shops of the Covered Bazaar, the biggest emporium in the world. Prices in the Covered Bazaar are about one-third cheaper than elsewhere in Istanbul. Bargaining in the bazaar is the rule, and it is enjoyed as much by shop owners as by visitors.

In addition to the Covered Bazaar, the main shopping centres of Istanbul include the modern mall of Galleria in Ataköy, near Atatürk International Airport; Istiklâl Caddesi in Beyoğlu; and the fashionable Nişantaşı-Osmanbey districts, in New Istanbul. Here is a selective list of shops and shopping centres in Istanbul where visitors can get the best buys:

Carpets can be irresistible

Carpets

BAZAAR 54
54 Nuruosmaniye Cad
Cağaloğlu
Tel: (0212) 5112150
Bazaar 54 has one of the largest selections of silk and wool carpets in the world, as well as Turkey's biggest jewellery centre and extensive collections of souvenirs. Prices tend to be higher if you go shopping in a group, so I advise you to go on your own. Bazaar 54 has served such famous clientele as former US presidents Richard Nixon and Jimmy Carter. Silk carpets are very expensive but a good investment.

GALLERY UGUR
Yerebatan Cad 15/1
Sultanahmet
Tel: (0212) 5206615/5206537
This shop specialises in handwoven wool carpets.

ŞENGÖR HALILARI
Takkeciler No 65-75-83
Kapalıçarşı
Tel: (0212) 5272192, 5224115
Şengor Halilari is one of the oldest and most venerated carpet sellers in the city.

ŞENGÖR HALILARI
Cumhuriyet Cad 47
Taksim
Tel: (0212) 2455919

Jewellery

ADLER MÜCEVHERAT
Hilton Hotel
Elmadağ
Tel: (0212) 2475990
This shop specialises in high-quality European products. Prices are expensive.

THE BROTHERS
Kapalıçarsı
Içbedesten
Şerifağa Sok No 30–31
Tel: (0212) 5284775
Hand-made Anatolian silver and gold jewellery. Prices are moderate.

Shopping Malls

GALLERIA
Ataköy
Shopping centre comprising some 600 shops, selling everything from leatherware and jewellery to carpets and books. Situated along the Sea of Marmara near the airport.

Department Stores

PRINTEMPS
Galleria
Ataköy
Tel: (0212) 5599850
Famous French department store.

Istanbul department store

Clothing

BEYMEN
Galleria
Ataköy
Tel: (0212) 5593250
Expensive but top-quality clothing here and in other shops operated by the same company.

BEYMEN
Halâskargazi Cad No 230
Osmanbey

VAKKO
Istiklâl Cad 123–125
Beyoğlu
Tel: (0212) 2514092
Expensive. Vakko products carry a certain snob appeal.

Souvenirs

SOFA SOUVENIRS
Nuruosmaniye Caddesi
Gündoğdu Iş Hanı No 42
Cağaloğlu
Tel: (0212) 5274142
Specialises in antiques and modern souvenirs as well as old and new miniature paintings.

Souvenirs for sale

Mementoes in Islamic script

Leatherware

DERIMOD
Halâskargazi Cad 222
Osmanbey
Tel: (0212) 2477481/2483648
Come here for stylish leather coats and jackets. Moderately priced.

DESA
Soğanağa Camii Sok
Akosman Işhanı No 2/4
Beyazıt
Tel: (0212) 5267248/5280018
Wide range of leather products from suitcases to belts, wallets and handbags. Other branches include:

DESA
Halâskargazi Cad No 216
Tel: (0212) 2476700

DESA
Galleria
Ataköy
Tel: (0212) 5599620

DESA
Istiklâl Cad 140
Beyoğlu
Tel: (0212) 2433786

UNIVERSAL COMPANY
Yerebatan Cad. 15 Kat 2
Sultanhamet
Tel: (0212) 5194684
Specialises in leather jackets. Good selection.

Calendar of Special Events

International Istanbul Film Festival: Istanbul is becoming the cultural centre of the Middle East. Scores of new foreign and Turkish films compete for top prizes during the International Istanbul Film Festival, held in March/April. It presents a good opportunity for film aficionados to view a wide spectrum of international movies at different cinema houses in Istanbul. Renowned film-makers and actors are invited as guests or as jury members, including Elia Kazan, Marcello Mastroianni, Carlos Saura and Andrej Wajda. Awards include the Golden Tulip, the grand prize of the festival; the Special Prize of the Jury, given as a specific contribution to a director, writer, actor, director of photography, composer or art director; and the Life Achievement Award, for any of the above categories.

International Istanbul Theatre Festival: Held in May/June and lasting for about a month, the International Istanbul Theatre Festival allows theatre troupes from a dozen countries to perform new plays before Turkish and international audiences. Each play is performed in the language of the country of the theatre troupe, often in the impressive setting of the Rumelihisarı fortress.

Patriotic fervour

The Conquest of Istanbul: On 29 May, municipal authorities celebrate the anniversary of the Turkish conquest of Istanbul in 1453, re-enacting battle scenes along the Byzantine walls between the Janissaries and the Byzantines and the holding of parades by the *Mehter* (Ottoman Marching Band).

International Istanbul Festival: A good time for culture vultures to visit the city is during the International Istanbul Festival (mid-June to end of July), when performances are given in 19 categories, including orchestra and chamber music, recitals, opera, ballet, modern dance, Turkish music concerts, jazz and pop concerts. Such famous orchestras as the New York Philharmonic Orchestra and the Berlin Symphony Orchestra perform. Pop and folk musicians, including Joan Baez, Tanita Tikaram, Sarah Vaughan and her trio, and Spyrogyra, are frequently featured, along with a line-up of top international jazz performers.

PRACTICAL Information

Airport from most major European, Asian and Middle Eastern cities. Turkish Airlines has an excellent network of local flights. There is no airport tax.

Here is a list of major airline offices in Istanbul:

AEROFLOT
Mete Cad 30
Taksim
Tel: (0212) 2434725

AIR FRANCE
Cumhuriyet Cad 1
Taksim
Tel: (0212) 2564356

ALIA AIRLINES
Cumhuriyet Cad 163 Kat2
Elmadağ
Tel: (0212) 2330744

ALITALIA
Cumhuriyet Cad Erk Apt 14/8
Elmadağ
Tel: (0212) 2313391/92

AMERICAN AIRLINES
Cumhuriyet Cad 47/2
Taksim
Tel: (0212) 2372003

AUSTRIAN AIRLINES
Sheraton Hotel
Askerocağı Cad 1
Taksim
Tel: (0212) 2322200

TRAVEL ESSENTIALS

Climate and When to Visit

Summers are warm in Istanbul and winters are mild and damp with plenty of rainfall. It occasionally snows. The best time to visit is May to June and September to October. It gets uncomfortably hot and humid July through August, forcing inhabitants to beaches along the Black Sea and Sea of Marmara to cool off.

Average temperatures are:

January: 5°C (41°F)
April: 11°C (52°F)
July: 23°C (73°F)
October: 16°C (61°F)

Air Transport

Turkish Airlines and many international carriers operate daily flights to Istanbul's Atatürk International

BALKAN AIRLINES
Cumhuriyet Cad
Gezi Dükkânları 8
Taksim
Tel: (0212) 2452456

BRITISH AIRWAYS
Cumhuriyet Cad 10
Elmadağ
Tel: (0212) 2341300

DELTA AIRLINES
Hilton Arcade
Cumhuriyet Cad
Harbiye
Tel: (0212) 2312339/45

EGYPT AIR
Cumhuriyet Cad 337–9 Kat 1
Harbiye
Tel: (0212) 231126

EL AL ISRAEL AIRLINES
Cumhuriyet Cad 187
Harbiye
Tel: (0212) 2465303

EMIRATES AIRLINES
Halaskârgazi Cad 69–71
Harbiye
Tel: (0212) 2323216

FINNAIR
Cumhuriyet Cad 26/A
Elmadağ
Tel: (0212) 2345130

GULFAIR
Cumhuriyet Cad 213
Harbiye
Tel: (0212) 2313450/54

IBERIAN AIRLINES
Topçu Cad
Uygun Apt 2/2
Taksim
Tel: (0212) 2551968

ISTANBUL AIRLINES
Cumhuriyet Cad 111 Kat 1
Elmadağ
Tel: (0212) 2317526

KLM ROYAL DUTCH AIRLINES
Abdi Ipekçi Cad 6–8
Nişantaşı
Tel: (0212) 2300311

KOREAN AIRLINES
Cumhuriyet Cad 8/7
Elmadağ
Tel: (0212) 2330410

LOT POLISH AIRLINES
Cumhuriyet Cad 91 Kat 2
Elmadağ
Tel: (0212) 2415749

LUFTHANSA
Maya Akan Center
Büyükdere Cad 100–102
Esentepe
Tel: (0212) 2881050

MIDDLE EAST AIRLINES
Cumburiyet Cad 30
Harbiye
Tel: (0212) 2482241

NORTHERN CYPRUS TURKISH AIRLINES
Sheraton Hotel
Elmadağ
Tel: (0212) 2465138

OLYMPIC AIRLINES
Cumhuriyet Cad 171/A
Elmadağ
Tel: (0212) 2465081

PAKISTAN INTERNATIONAL AIRLINES
Cumhuriyet Cad
Darhan 203
Tel: (0212) 2330571

SABENA
Topçular Cad 2/1
Taksim
Tel: (0212) 2547254

SAUDI ARABIAN AIRLINES
Cumhuriyet Cad 33
Taksim
Tel: (0212) 2564800

SCANDINAVIAN AIRLINES SYSTEM
Cumhuriyet Cad 26/A
Elmadağ
Tel: (0212) 2466075

SINGAPORE AIRLINES
Halaskangazi Cad 113
Harbiye
Tel: (0212) 2323706

Airport–City Links

A regular bus shuttle service operates between the Turkish Airlines Terminal in Şişhane, central Istanbul, and Ataturk International Airport. However, the fastest and most comfortable way to travel to and from the airport is by taxi. You should leave your hotel about two hours before your flight.

Road Transport

Istanbul is only three hours from the Bulgarian and Greek borders, linked by modern highways. Several private Turkish bus companies operate between European cities and Istanbul. These buses are the cheapest mode of transport to Istanbul from Central

Europe. There are regular bus services to most Turkish cities from Istanbul's Bayrampaşa Bus Terminal (*Oto Gar*) on the European side of the Bosphorus, and Harem Bus Terminal on the Asian side.

Sea Transport

Istanbul is a port of call for many European luxury liners.

Rail Transport

The city is a major destination for European trains. The city has two rail terminals, Sirkeci terminal, on the European side of Istanbul between the Galata Bridge and the Topkapı Palace, and Haydarpaşa terminal, on the Asian side. From Haydarpaşa trains leave for many cities in Anatolia by train.

Car Rental

AVIS
Atatürk International Airport
Domestic Flights Terminal
Tel: (0212) 5731452/5733870
Foreign Flights Terminal
Tel: (0212) 6630646
Hilton Hotel
Tel: (0212) 2487752
Bağdat Caddesi
Alageyik Sok 196/4
Kadıköy
Tel: (0216) 3553665

EUROPCAR
Head Office
Cumhuriyet 47/2

Taksim, Istanbul
Tel: (0212) 2547788
Fax: (0212) 2507649
Talimhane, Topçu Sok Cad 1
Taksim, Istanbul
Tel: 2547799
Atatürk International Airport
International Flights Terminal
Tel: (0212) 6630746
Domestic Flights Terminal
Tel: (0212) 5741908
Bağdat Cad 204
Giftehavuzlar, Kadıköy
Tel: (0216) 3603333

HERTZ
Atatürk International Airport
Tel: (0212) 6630807
Cumhuriyet Cad 295
Harbiye
Tel: (0212) 2416914
Fax: (0212) 2329260

Visas

Provided they have a valid passport, nationals of the following countries do not need a visa for visits of up to three months: Australia, Austria, Bahamas, Fiji, Finland, France, Gambia, Germany, Gibraltar, Greece, Hong Kong, Iran, Iceland, Italy, Jamaica, Japan, Kenya, Kuwait, Mauritius, Morocco, Norway, Netherlands, New Zealand, Oman, Saudi Arabia, Seychelles, Singapore, Spain, Switzerland, Trinidad and Tobago, Tunisia, Uganda, United Arab Emirates and USA.

British citizens require a visa which enables them to stay for three months.

Nationals of South Korea, Portugal, Rumania and the Czech and Slovak Republics do not require a visa for visits up to two months (provided they hold a valid passport). Nationals of Malaysia may stay up

to 15 days under the same conditions.

Nationals of any other countries must obtain a visa.

Money Matters

Most Turkish banks cash travellers' cheques and foreign currency. Exchange rates are posted daily in front of the banks. Banking hours are 8.30am–12 noon and 1.30–4pm, Monday to Friday. Some private exchange offices remain open on the weekends. The national currency is the Turkish *lira* (TL). The *lira* comes in coins of 500TL, 1,000TL, 2,500TL, and 5,000TL; and in notes of 10,000TL, 20,000TL, 50,000TL, 100,000TL, 250,000TL, 500,000TL and 1 millionTL.

Foreign currency, including traveller's cheques, can be cashed at most hotels and banks. But the best exchange rates are available at money changers (*döviz büfesi*), which are abundant in Istanbul.

Clothing

Light clothing is recommended in summer, as it can get very hot. In the winter months from November to March, sweaters and overcoats should be brought. Comfortable shoes are needed for long, leisurely strolls.

Electricity

The electricity in Turkey is of the 220-volt, 50-cycle variety. The two-round-prong European plug will usually work here.

GETTING ACQUAINTED
Time Differences

Turkish Standard Time is seven hours ahead of Eastern Standard Time and two hours ahead of Greenwich Mean Time.

HAŞET KITABEVI
Istiklâl Cad 469
Beyoğlu
Tel: (0212) 2449470/2434326

LIBRAIRIE DE PERA
Galip Dede Cad 22
Tünel
Tel: (0212) 2454998/2523078

HOURS & HOLIDAYS

Business Hours

Government offices are open from 8.30 am–12 noon and 1.30–5 pm.

Public Holidays

January 1: New Year's Day
April 23: National Sovereignty and Children's Day
May 19: Youth and Sports Holiday
August 30: Victory Day
October 29: Republic Day
In addition, there are two Muslim holidays whose dates vary from year to year:
Şeker Bayramı (Sweet Holiday), follows Ramadan
Kurban Bayramı (Feast of the Sacrifice)

ACCOMMODATION

Old Istanbul

US$150 and Up

MERIT ANTIQUE ISTANBUL
Tel: (0212) 5139300
Fax: (0212) 5126390

US$90 and Up

HOLIDAY INN
Ataköy Marina, Sahil Yolu
34710 Ataköy
Tel: (0212) 5604110
Fax: (0212) 5594905

PRESIDENT HOTEL
Tiyatro Cad 25, Beyazıt
Tel: (0212) 5166980
Fax: (0212) 5166999

TOPKAPI ERESIN HOTEL
Millet Cad
Topkapı
Tel: (0212) 6311212
Fax: (0212) 5332810

US$75 and Up

AYA SOFYA PANSIYONLARI
Soğukçeşme Sok
Sultanahmet
Tel: (0212) 5133660
Fax: (0212) 5133669

KARIYE HOTEL
Kariye Camii Sok 18, Edirnekapı
Tel: (0212) 5348414
Fax: (0212) 5216631

YEŞIL EV
Kabasakal Cad 5, Sultanahmet
Tel: (0212) 5176785/5286764

US$50 and Up

HOTEL AVICENNA
Mimar Mehmet Ağa Cad, Amiral Tafdil Sok No 31–33, Sultanahmet

Tel: (0212) 5170550
Fax: (0212) 5166555

A VEZIRHAN HOTEL
Alemadar Cad 7
Sultanahmet
Tel: (0212) 5112414/5112319

HOTEL AYASOFYA
Küçükayasofya Mah, Demirci Reşit
Sokak 28, Sultanahmet
Tel: (0212) 5169446/5173776

HOTEL HIPPODROME
Mimar Mehmetağa Cad 17
Sultanahmet
Tel: (0212) 5160268/5176889

HOTEL SOKULLU PAŞA
Ishakpaşa Mah, Mehmetpaşa Sok 10
Sultanahmet
Tel: (0212) 5123756/57/58

HOTEL SUMENGEN
Mimar Mehmet Ağa Cad
Amiral Tafdil Sok 21, Sultanahmet
Tel: (0212) 5176869/5176872

KÜÇÜK AYA SOFYA HOTEL
Küçük Ayasofya Mah, Şehit
Mehmetpaşa Sok 25, Sultanahmet
Tel: (0212) 5161988
Fax: (0212) 5168356

New Istanbul
US$150 and Up

CONRAD HOTEL
Barbaros Bulvarı, Yıldız Cad
Beşiktaş
Tel: (0212) 2273000
Fax: (0212) 2596667

HILTON HOTEL
Cumhuriyet Cad, Harbiye
Tel: (0212) 2314650
Fax: (0212) 2404165

HYATT REGENCY ISTANBUL
Taşkişla Cad
Tel: (0212) 22570000
Fax (0212) 2257007

MÖVENPICK HOTEL
Büyükdere Cad 49, Üçyol Mevkii
Maslak
Tel: (0212) 2850900
Fax: 2850951/52

SWISS HOTEL THE BOSPHORUS
Bayıldım Cad No 2, Maçka
Tel: (0212) 2590101
Fax: (0212) 2590105

US$120 and Up

DIVAN HOTEL
Cumhuriyet Cad 2, Taksim
Tel: (0212) 2314100
Fax: (0212) 2488527

THE MARMARA ISTANBUL
Taksim
Tel: (0212) 2514696
Fax: (0212) 2440509

PERA PALAS HOTEL
Meşrutiyet Cad 98/100
Tepebaşı
Tel: (0212) 2514560
Fax: (0212) 2514089

RICHMOND HOTEL
Istikklal Cad 445
Beyoğlu
Tel: (0212) 2525460
Fax: (0212) 2529707

US$100 and Up

BÜYÜK SÜRMELI HOTEL
Saatçıbayırı Sok No 3, Gayrettepe
Tel: (0212) 2721160

DEDEMAN HOTEL
Yıldızposta Cad 50, Esentepe
Tel: (0212) 2748800

ETAP ISTANBUL
Mesrutiyet Cad, Tepebaşı
Tel: (0212) 2514646

MAÇKA HOTEL
Eytam Cad 35, Teşvikiye
Tel: (0212) 2343200
Fax: (0212) 28002

Near the Airport
US$120 and Up
HOLIDAY INN CROWNE PLAZA
Sahil Yolu
34710 Ataköy
Tel: (0212) 560 8100

US$100 and Up

ÇINAR HOTEL
Fener Mevkii, Yeşilköy
Tel: (0212) 5732910
Fax: (0212) 573501

On the Bosphorus
US$150 and Up
ÇIRAĞAN PALAS KEMPINSKI
Çırağan Cad 84
80700 Beşiktaş
Tel: (0212) 2583377
Fax: (0212) 2596686/87

US$100 and Up
BÜYÜK TARABYA HOTEL
Tarabya
Tel: (0212) 2621000/2620710
Fax: (0212) 2622260

HIDIV KASRI
Çubuklu
Tel: (0216) 3312651/3224042
Fax: (0216) 3223434

ACKNOWLEDGMENTS

Photography	
Cover	**Şemsi Güner**
Backcover	**Hans Höfer**
15, 33, 57T, 86T, 89, 97, 112T, 114, 118M, 120B	**Nevzat Çakır**
26T, 30, 59, 90T, 119	**Metin Demirsar**
73, 78B, 85, 90B, 92T, 106T, 118B, 120T	**Mehmet Erdur**
28T, 54T	**Nermi Erdur**
10, 24T, 26B, 27T, 31, 50, 53, 54B, 55T, 45T,	**Ara Güler**
58T, 58B, 60–61B, 67B, 70T, 74B, 79, 81T, 82T,	
82B, 84T, 92B, 96T, 100T, 103B, 108T,	
108B, 111T, 111B, 112B, 116T, 118T	
3, 12, 17, 22, 23, 24B, 25, 27B, 28, 29B,	**Şemsi Güner**
29T, 32, 38, 39, 41, 42–43, 44, 45, 46, 47, 52,	
56–57B, 61, 62, 63B, 64, 68, 70–71B, 72, 74T,	
76T, 78T, 86B, 94, 96B, 98, 100B, 102, 103T,	
107, 109, 110, 113	
8/9	**Kısmet/FOG**
6, 99, 101	**Mehmet Kısmet**
34, 35T, 35B, 36, 49, 60T, 63T, 66, 67T,	**Enis Özbank**
71B, 75, 76B, 81T, 83T, 84B, 106B, 116B	
2/3	**Şakır/FOG**
56B, 77, 105	**Unidiabank**
48, 87, 88, 104, 110	**Phil Wood**
Handwriting	**V.Barl**
Cover Design	**Klaus Geisler**
Cartography	**Berndtson & Berndtson**